MW00457611

ISRAEL EDUCATION MATTERS

A 21ST CENTURY PARADIGM FOR JEWISH EDUCATION

Lisa D. Grant and Ezra M. Kopelowitz

Peoplehood in Practice Series

Published by the Center for Jewish Peoplehood Education

Jerusalem, Israel

Peoplehood in Practice is a publication series focused on education for identity, connection and commitment to the Jewish people.

Peoplehood in Practice focuses on the point at which academia meets the field. Publications represent the highest levels of academic and intellectual research and thinking for a target audience of academics, intellectuals, community leaders, educators and practitioners who are concerned with the practical questions of fortifying collective Jewish life in our times. The publications address those who are interested in understanding long term processes of change taking place in the world Jewish community *and* by those who are committed to the day to day task of building collective Jewish belonging in our open society.

We dedicate this book to a primary source of our Israel education, our parents, Murray z"l and Marilyn Grant and Natie and Brenda Kopelowitz. Their love for Israel has inspired us on an infinitely rewarding and always complicated journey of which this book is a part.

LIBRARY OF CONGRESS CARD CATALOGING-IN-PUBLICATION DATA

Printed in the United States of America

First Printing, 2012

ISBN – 10 0-985-81190-0

ISBN – 13 978-0-985-81190-7

The Center for Jewish Peoplehood Education
The Schecter Institute
P.O.B. 16080
Jerusalem, Israel 91160
www.jpeoplehood.org/

The Center for Jewish Peoplehood Education

Founded in 2011, CJPE seeks to create and sustain a vibrant and thriving Jewish People whose institutions nurture belonging and commitment to the Jewish collective enterprise for the purpose of enriching Jewish life and making the world a better place. CJPE addresses the challenges of Jewish Peoplehood education, offering institutions and individuals the resources and support to obtain professional development, content and programmatic development or general Peoplehood conceptual and educational consulting.

Cover design by Avi Maidenberg

10 9 8 7 6 5 4 3 2 1

CONTENTS

About the Authors...1

Foreword.. 3

Acknowledgements 4

Israel Education Matters 5

The Principles of Israel Education.. 8

Why Israel Education? A Look at the Changing Nature of Collective Jewish Belonging..14

Three Dimensions of Israel Education: "Integrate," "Complicate" and "Connect"..22

I. Integrate: Making Israel Part of Ongoing Jewish Life 26

Vignette 1: Five Dimensions of Israel in a Jewish school..................29

Vignette 2: JCDS – Integrating Israel through Hebrew......................37

Vignette 3: Building Leadership for Engagement with Israel in Synagogues 42

Vignette 4: Israel travel – On the need for follow-up strategies.......51

Notes for Educators on Integrating Israel..................................57

II. Complicate: From Reflexive Commitment to Mature Love.....63

Vignette 1: When the Jewish People and Israel Conflict...................70

Vignette 2: Complicating Israel in the Classroom and on the Road...76

Vignette 3: Complicating Israel at a Community Jewish Day School..86

Vignette 4: Beyond the B-word. Listening to High School Students Talk about Israel. Author: Alex Pomson.......................................92

Notes for Educators on Complicating Israel.............................. 103

III. Connect: Building Social Networks Between Jews Inside and Outside of Israel 114

Vignette 1: The Mifgash.. 118

Vignette 2: People-to-People Strategies for Israel Education at Summer Camp 123

Vignette 3: Yachdav/School-to-School Israel-Diaspora Virtual Mifgash 130

Notes for Educators on Connecting to Israel 137

Concluding Case Study – Looking at How Integrate, Complicate, and Connect Come Together at Camp Harlam. Co-authored with Vicki Tuckman 144

Conclusion 167

References 175

Index 188

ABOUT THE AUTHORS

Lisa D. Grant

Lisa is Professor of Jewish Education at Hebrew Union College – Jewish Institute of Religion (New York campus) *and a Fellow at the Center for Jewish Peoplehood Education*. She holds an M.B.A. in public management from the University of Massachusetts and a Ph.D. in Jewish Education from the Jewish Theological Seminary. Prior to joining the HUC faculty, she served as Evaluation and Pilot Project Manager at the Melton Research Center for Jewish Education. Her research and teaching interests focus on adult Jewish learning and the place of Israel in American Jewish life. For the past five years, she has been part of the faculty and planning team of an HUC-Mandel Foundation initiative that focuses on developing visionary rabbinic leadership with a strong grounding in and commitment to Israel and the Jewish People.

Lisa is co-editor of the International Handbook of Jewish Education (Springer, 2011).   Recent publications related to Israel and Jewish Peoplehood include, Grant, Lisa D. "Pluralistic Approaches to Israel Education," Journal of Jewish Education, Vol. 77:1 (Winter, 2011); Grant, Lisa and Ravid Shlomi, "Creating a Sustainable Sense of Peoplehood: Towards a Pedagogy of Commitment," Jewish Educational Leadership, Vol. 9:2, (Winter, 2011); Grant, Lisa D. "Sacred Vision, Complex Reality: Navigating the Tensions in Israel Education," Jewish Educational Leadership, Vol. 7:1, (Fall, 2008); Grant, Lisa D. and Marmur, Michael, "The Place of Israel in the Identity of Reform Jews," in Danny Ben Moshe, editor, Israel, World Jewry, and Identity. London: Sussex Academic Press (2007).

Lisa lives in Brooklyn, NY with her husband, Billy Weitzer.   She has two young adult children.

Ezra M. Kopelowitz

Ezra is a sociologist specializing in the Jewish world and Jewish Education. He is CEO of Research Success Technologies (ReST) and a Fellow at the Center for Jewish Peoplehood Education. Ezra is a pioneer in research on Jewish Peoplehood, developing intellectual frameworks and conducting applied research for the purpose of advancing the field on matters pertaining to collective Jewish identity and Jewish education. Recent publications include: Building Jewish Peoplehood: Change and Challenge, Academic Studies Press. (2008, co-edited *with Menachem Revivi*); Cultural Education-Cultural Sustainability: Minority, Diaspora, Indigenous and Ethno-Religious Groups in Multicultural Societies, Routledge (2008, co-edited *with Zvi Beckerman*); A Framework for Strategic Thinking about Jewish Peoplehood (Position paper commissioned by the Nadav Fund. Tel Aviv. 2007).

Ezra was born in South Africa, raised in the United States and has lived in Israel since 1990. He lives on Kibbutz Hannaton in the Galilee. He is married to Debbie with four children.

FOREWORD

There is a tremendous growth of interest in education for collective Jewish belonging, often focused in the areas of Jewish Peoplehood and Israel education. Despite the interest and the many individuals and organizations that are now working in this area, the field is still in a nascent state. As the field of Peoplehood education evolves and develops, so does the need for thought papers and scholarship. Currently, there is a very limited body of research that explores the purposes and practices of Peoplehood education in general and Israel education in particular. This gap impedes the development of educational programs and materials, not to mention the pedagogic conversation about nurturing Peoplehood in practice.

Israel Education Matters is the first book in the *Peoplehood in Practice* publication series, which focuses on education for identity, connection and commitment to Israel and the Jewish people. This book represents an integrated paradigm that we at the Center for Jewish Peoplehood Education wish for the field. *Israel Education Matters* focuses on the point at which academia meets the field. The book at once meets the highest standards of academic and intellectual research and thinking, but will be read not only by academics and intellectuals, but also by community leaders, educators and practitioners who are concerned with the practical work-a-day challenges of fortifying collective Jewish life in our times.

Our hope is that this book will be read both by those interested in understanding long term processes of change taking place in the world Jewish community and by those who are committed to the day to day task of building collective Jewish belonging in an open society.

Shlomi Ravid
Director, Center for Jewish Peoplehood Education
Jerusalem, Israel
September, 2012

ACKNOWLEDGEMENTS

We would like thank our colleagues, researchers on Jewish education and Jewish educators with whom we have shared the intellectual journey of which this book is a part. As we describe in the book, the paradigm of Israel Education for which we advocate is part of broader shifts occurring in Jewish education and the Jewish world more broadly. It has been our privilege to have colleagues and clients who are invested in the future of the Jewish people and dedicated to pushing forward the field and us through conversation and collaboration. In particular, we'd like to thank the following individuals whose input and support has been particularly influential: Ami Bouganim, Steven M. Cohen, Elan Ezrachi, Alick Isaacs, Rachel Korazim, David Mittelberg, Alex Pomson, Varda Rafaeli, Shlomi Ravid, Ted Sasson, Loren Sykes, Vicki Tuckman, and Yehudit Werchow.

ISRAEL EDUCATION MATTERS

In recent years, the question "why does (or should) Israel matter to Jews who live outside of Israel?" has been raised in various ways by Jewish leaders worldwide and in the general Jewish press. This question is precipitated by a variety of political, social, and cultural factors that have led to a vigorous and heated debate about whether or not young American Jews are growing increasingly distant from Israel. Typically, the debate focuses on claims and counter-claims about how a trip to Israel might cure the ills of assimilation and intermarriage or how the American Jewish "street" accepts or rejects Israel's political policies. Rarely, however, does the debate address the fact that Israel matters because it is a core element of Judaism and the collective Jewish experience wherever it is lived.

Israel matters because it is an integral aspect of collective Jewish life, regardless of political or religious orientation. The more richly one is involved in Jewish life, the more likely one is to be engaged with one or more of Israel's multiple historical, religious, political, social, and cultural dimensions. In other words, these many dimensions of *Am, Torah, Eretz,* and *Medinah* are indispensable resources for collective and individual Jewish life. Thus, if one cares about preserving and building a sense of mutual responsibility and connection among Jews and the Jewish People, Israel education becomes an integral component of how to foster and sustain those connections.

This book documents a new strategy for Israel education emerging in the field among a group of thinkers and educators who share an educational worldview premised upon what we describe here as a "paradigm of mutuality and meaning." This approach sets no pre-conditions for where one's cultural, religious, or political positions lie in regard to Israeli governmental policy or action. It presumes that the symbols, beliefs, expressions, and actions of being a Jew are part of a common weave out of which Jewish belonging is knit. The connection to Israel must begin with that complex weave. Just as Israel is an integral component of Jewish existence, so too must Israel education be an integral part of a holistic Jewish education. Understanding Israel as integral, however, does not preclude a range of different personal commitments, connections, and expressions. Just as all would agree that Shabbat is core to Jewish experience but that different Jews observe Shabbat in different ways, the same can be said for Israel. There is no one right way to engage with Israel, but engaging is an essential aspect of Jewish experience. Just as educators strive to help Jews find meaning in Shabbat and cultivate the motivation, knowledge or skills that enable them to be with other Jews on Shabbat; so should they work to help Jews engage with Israel, each on their own terms, yet as part of the collective Jewish project.

For over a decade, the authors of this book have together and separately, been among the researchers investigating the question of "why Israel matters?" We conduct academic and policy oriented research on a wide variety of Jewish institutional venues, including Israel programs, synagogues, camps, schools and other educational settings. From project to project we can observe the historical significance of the evolution of "Israel education." Today, Israel education is not just an educational strategy, but rather, is a looking glass into the very core of Jewish belonging or the manner in which Jews fashion a connection to the Jewish People.

Israel as a resource

"Israel education" is built on an understanding that Israel is a "major resource" for Jewish life. Yet, unlike the classic Zionism of Israel's founders and to which many continue to subscribe, we regard Israel as a center, but not *the* center of Jewish life. Jewish life in the Diaspora may well exist without Israel, but in so doing, that Jewish life would be less. The same is true for Jewish life in Israel vis-à-vis the Diaspora. The existence of each strengthens the other.

Understanding Israel as a vital, but not necessarily central resource recognizes the existence and thriving of Jewish centers all over the world. As one of the largest Jewish communities, Israel certainly serves a major hub in the network of global Jewish communities. Yet, the same can be said of American Jewry. Each serves as a vital communal, social, and intellectual resource for enabling a Jewish life capable of thriving in contemporary society.

Worldwide, Jewish communities each develop in their own unique ways. When we are concerned with the relationship of those communities to one another, Jewish Peoplehood remains an ongoing and vital reality. The role of Israel as an educational resource for Diaspora communities within the global network is the focus of this book. In a different book we might look at the Diaspora as a resource for Israeli Jews.

The problem

The challenge for Diaspora Jewish educators is the fact that much of Israel education currently consists of symbolic experiences predicated on ceremonial, episodic and rather superficial encounters. While the symbolic is vital, it is not enough. A relationship with Israel that rests on ceremony alone keeps Israel at a distance and limits any active sense of mutuality. In addition, symbols and ceremony often are simplistic and avoid problematizing or over-complicating, in order to produce a strong emotional tie. While a successful ceremony and strong feeling of emotional connection may be a first step in binding participants as a group to a greater whole, meaningful engagement necessitates going well beyond ceremony and symbol, toward nuanced and textured experiences, based on real, rather than solely symbolic interactions. A balanced approach to Israel education should include dimensions of both symbolic and critical engagement rooted in the social reality of individuals' lives.

THE PRINCIPLES OF ISRAEL EDUCATION

Israel education is a way into understanding what it means to be a Jew in the contemporary world. In this book we provide a synthesis of our work in order to help advance a deeper understanding of a new paradigm for Jewish life, which the concept of "Israel education" represents.

The mutuality and meaning paradigm

The "mutuality and meaning paradigm" focuses on "why Israel matters" for the individual Jew and illustrates how answers to that question inform Jewish education.

The mutuality and meaning paradigm stands in sharp contrast to a family of strategies commonly known as "Israel advocacy." In the field, Israel advocates are understood to be those whose stated agenda is to support and defend Israel. This represents a classic Zionist approach that assumes Jews have a strong and positive connection to Israel; all that is needed is to convince others to do the same. In the advocacy context, education is about imparting knowledge about Israel and skills that train the advocate to defend Israel. The educational effort focuses on outcomes that impact "the other," and not on the individual Jew who is the Israel advocate. As a result, the most basic and fundamental question of why Israel matters for each individual Jew is ignored: "Why Israel for me?"

While important and indeed vital work, Israel advocacy alone is far too narrow an approach to tackle the core dictum that guides our work: "Israel matters." Why does Israel matter to contemporary Jewry? How does the answer to that question inform the work of Jewish education? How does the answer to that question capture the broadest range of Diaspora Jewry's cultural, religious, and political orientations and the role of Israel?

By situating Israel education within the broader questions of Jewish life, this book addresses the "why Israel for me" question head on. What does it take to enable Jews to engage with Israel in a way that they find meaningful?

Two foundational ideas

Two foundational ideas undergird our understanding of how Israel education can contribute to a broader vision for promoting active Jewish life. First, we cannot presume a commitment on the part of individual Jews to the Jewish collective. We must instead begin with the individual and work out to the group. We cannot assume the group; we must actively nurture it. Secondly, we understand life in general and Jewish life in particular as dynamic, fluid, and multi-dimensional. To be Jewish means living in a larger world, where being Jewish is but one of many identities people move between, mixing, matching, and merging.

1. Begin with the individual, work out to the group

The concept of Jewish belonging that Israel education offers is not about socializing an individual into a clear set of group practices to support Israel; nor, is it about setting boundaries that determines who is in and out. Rather, Israel education assumes that in contemporary society, collective belonging is moving away from clear collectives with prescribed boundaries to more fluid social networks in which individuals move and maintain multiple affiliations. One can be Jewish *and* American, live in Atlanta, San Francisco, or New York *and* feel a deep connection to Israel and not regard these multiple points of reference in mutually exclusive tension with one another. The same is true of an Israeli, who lives in Tel Aviv *and* feels a part of the Jewish People, or a Jew who is religious *and* has non-Jewish friends. We no longer operate with the assumption of national, religious or ethnic affiliations demanding total allegiance.

Jews will opt into the Jewish People, when each individual sees the choice of membership as bringing depth and richness to life. This in turn begets questions which require answers, such as: "Do I seek a life partner who is Jewish?" "Should I belong to a synagogue and/or other Jewish institutions in my local Jewish community?" "Do I support the welfare of Jews who live elsewhere?" And, "what is my relationship to Israel?" Answers to these questions, and many others are integral to living a Jewish life. One cannot be Jewish without grappling with them. However, no one will grapple with them if they do not experience a social, emotional, and intellectual process that establishes the questions as relevant for life.

2. Being Jewish is a lived experience

Life is first and foremost social and interactive - "life is with people." In order for Israel education to engage the hearts and minds of Jews, it must become part of the social and interactive fabric of life as people live it. Yet, for many Diaspora Jews, Israel is not at all connected to the dynamic nature of their lives. Rather, Israel remains a mythical or symbolic entity, a static presence in their lives, found, if at all, only in ceremonies, liturgy, and holidays. The same holds true for many Israeli Jews in terms of their understanding of the role of Jewish life in Israeli society and the connection of Israeli Jews to Jews who live outside of Israel.

Israel education at its best enables the educator and learner to engage Israel on two levels: 1) The ceremonial level, where Israel serves as a unifying force for the Jewish People. In ceremonies we embrace that which is most inspiring in order to bring out the best in ourselves and in our service to each other; and, 2) Israel on the level of real life, where the country is both inspiring and often heartbreakingly real, incredibly frustrating, filled with contradictions, disappointments, moral ambiguities and complexities that challenge us on a daily basis.

This two dimensional experience of Israel, is similar for all facets of Jewish life. For example, the study of *Torah* – it too is endowed with holiness, a unifying force, and a source of inspiration for doing justice in the world. But, it too is filled with contradictions, ambiguities, and complexities that challenge us. And one can certainly say the same thing about God. Indeed, each of the three defining pillars of Judaism – God, *Torah*, and Israel has multiple sides and many interpretations, all of which invite Jews to struggle with meaning and purpose and to engage in Jewish life.

In this sense, to be a member of the Jewish People is no different than the challenge of living in a family or a community. We don't identify or enjoy every moment, but we do crave the benefits and experience the love of being part of a greater collective. Such is the complexity of life of what we will refer to in this book as "mature love."

Responding to the pitfalls of unreflective love

It may well be that Israel Education's embrace of the complexity of Jewish belonging and of Israel within that weave, flies in the face of many educators who strive to instill a "love" of Israel. While Israel educators embrace the complexity of Jewish life and as such the complexity of Israel's place in Jewish life, many educators fear that revealing too many of Israel's complexities may alienate students and undermine formation of a strong Jewish identity. Indeed, a strong argument can be made for the need to cultivate a sense of connection and commitment before inviting a more critical approach. Yet, a conventional approach to education about Israel that promotes and perhaps even demands an unreflective love, may ultimately leave Israel as a superficial, peripheral and even an alienating aspect of American Jewish life (Ackerman 1996; Chazan 2005; Grant, 2007, 2008).

Recent trends in Israel education reflect awareness of the pitfalls of such unreflective love. For example, nearly all of the papers presented at a January, 2007 Israel Education Think Tank convened by the Melton Centre for Jewish Education at the Hebrew University in Jerusalem, noted that old ways of teaching Israel were inadequate and outmoded for dealing with a multi-layered, dynamic, and complex reality that often conflicts with many of the foundational myths that still comprise the core of what is being taught in schools, camps, and Israel trips for Diaspora Jews. Many of the papers went further, saying that we need to move away from a classical Zionist paradigm that keeps

Israel at the center and implies, either implicitly or explicitly, that Israel is the only place where one can live life fully as a Jew.

Similarly, in the February/March 2008 issue of *Sh'ma* dedicated to Israel education, many writers directly criticized an approach to education about Israel that focuses exclusively on advocacy or unquestioned support of the State. Virtually all agreed that the role of the educator is to help learners grapple with complex issues and questions and to develop an informed opinion that they can support. This necessitates moving away from teaching solely myths and symbols and sharing more of Israel's "blemishes and flaws" (Geffen, 2008, p. 4), shifting to a "commitment and critique" paradigm (Perlman, 2008, p. 17) or engaging in what Robbie Gringras (2008) calls "hugging and wrestling" with Israel (p. 19).

Likewise, the Fall 2008 issue of *Jewish Educational Leadership* devoted to Israel education contains numerous articles challenging educators to re-examine and rethink the teaching of Israel. As Daniel Margolis writes:

We and our communities should re-examine our ideological commitments, how we, in all our diversity, understand and relate to the basic Jewish core texts and ideas that put Zion and Israel – Land and People – at the center of our tradition and history. A necessary center, yes, but still an insufficient one to define us as complete Jews. We will each understand these root sources differently and relate to contemporary Israel differently, but from that re-examination, a new, contemporary articulation of our stances will emerge (Margolis, 2008, p. 20).

The April 2010 issue of Sh'ma contains another set of articles that explores the question of what it means to be a loyal Jew and when and to what extent is critique of Israel allowed in the Jewish public square. This debate is playing out on an ongoing basis in the popular Jewish press and numerous blogs dealing with American Jewish life. One significant trigger was Peter Beinart's June, 2010 *New York Review of Books* article "The Failure of the American Jewish Establishment" that sparked a fascinating flurry of exchanges between left, right, and center to support or condemn his assertion that younger American Jews are disenchanted with both Israel and the American Jewish establishment that blindly supports it without, as he claims, regard for the dramatic erosion of civil rights and democratic values that is taking place in Israeli society today. Beinart advocates for an "uncomfortable Zionism" that demands engagement with morally difficult questions relating to the "ethical use of Jewish power" (p. 2). To be sure, this article and the numerous responses it provoked are proof positive that the issue of critical engagement is becoming part of normative American Jewish discourse today.

WHY ISRAEL EDUCATION?
A LOOK AT THE CHANGING NATURE OF COLLECTIVE JEWISH BELONGING

Three trends contribute to the attention being paid to Israel education today. One relates to broad patterns of historical change having to do with Jewish belonging, the other two relate to a survivalist orientation in Jewish education that grows out of both perceived and real threats to the Jewish future.

1. The Evolution of Jewish Belonging

Until the mid-twentieth century, most American Jews lived in ethnic enclaves, usually tightly knit urban communities where the social and cultural boundaries between Jews and non-Jews were reinforced through informal processes of everyday life (Diner, Shandler, & Wenger, 2000; Portes & Manning 2012). The mass exodus of America's Jews out of the ethnic neighborhood to suburbia in the 1940s, 50s, and 60s, ushered in an era in which the concept of "affiliation" came to define Jewish belonging.

Beyond informal friendships, Jews in suburbia formally associated themselves with Jewish organizations in order to take part in Jewish communal life. An example of the shift can be seen in how the role of the synagogue changed as more and more Jews moved outside of ethnic enclaves. In the urban setting, the synagogue was one node in the individual's larger Jewish communal experience, and hence only accessed for religious purposes narrowly defined. In suburbia the synagogue became a communal hub, effectively offering a replacement to the lost ethnic neighborhood. Whereas, in the ethnic urban neighborhood a synagogue's physical space was devoted to the purpose of prayer or religious learning, in suburbia the "synagogue center" became a multi-dimensional institution offering a large spectrum of services. Only approximately 10% or so of the synagogue center's building was used for prayer. The synagogue changed from a specifically religious institution to a primarily communal organization (Kaufman, 1999).

Suburbanization of American Jewry began a process where collective Jewish belonging became a choice. In other words, a person must choose an affiliation with a Jewish organization in order to actively associate with the Jewish community. For the first generation out of the ethnic enclaves, affiliation with Jewish institutions was for most an obvious choice. To take membership in a Jewish organization was an act of recreating the Jewish neighborhood. Jewish organizations were built on the assumption that Jews, raised in pre-WWII ethnic Jewish neighborhoods, saw an inherent value for socializing with other Jews and hence would seek affiliation with Jewish communal organizations.

Many Jews who came of age in suburbia no longer saw as obvious the need to seek out Jewish friendships by affiliating with Jewish organizations. Whereas the parents grew up on the streets of city neighborhoods playing with their Jewish friends, the children attended suburban schools in which Jews and non-Jews mixed freely. The parents wanted to recreate the social experience of their youth by joining Jewish institutions, but in an increasingly multi-cultural society that offered open-access to Jews, their children asked why was it necessary to restrict their social networks to Jews alone.

Starting in the 1970s, outward signs of assimilation increased, with the most visible being increased rates of intermarriage. In organizational terms, many of the affiliation era institutions stagnated, both in terms of membership numbers and in terms of the responsive nature of the model for Jewish life they offered their constituents. While the synagogue and community center models were appropriate for the first generation of Jews in suburbia, they became increasingly irrelevant to large swaths of the younger generations of American Jewry who were not affiliating with established Jewish organizations (Cohen 1998; Cohen & Eisen, 2000; Cohen & Kelman, 2007).

Israel education serves as a case study for the transformative changes occurring within the institutions created to serve the Jews who left their ethnic neighborhoods for suburbia and new forms of organized Jewish life, which are now appearing to provide younger generations of Jews alternative venues for opting into Jewish life (Kopelowitz & Ravid, 2010). The common denominator is an attempt to create compelling forms of Jewish community, or "meaningful Jewish engagement" which provide the gateway into active membership in the Jewish People for a generation who did not grow up in a Diaspora ethnic enclave. Since so much of the way Diaspora Jews relate to Israel is through Jewish communal organizations, questions arise regarding the impact of weakened institutional ties to attachment to Israel.

The changes are part of broader trends in religious and communal practice in general, where identity is defined far more by personal choice than any adherence to a communal norm (Bellah et al., 1985; Putnam, 2001; Roof, 2001; Wuthnow, 2010). Like their non-Jewish counterparts, most Jews increasingly prefer the personal over the collective, the episodic over the regular, and the grass-roots over the institutional. They define their own personal style of Judaism, choosing whether, how, and when to connect (Cohen & Kelman, 2006; Ukeles, Miller, & Beck, 2006). Most Israel education initiatives, as with many other educational initiatives in the Jewish world are trying to grapple with this broader phenomenon.

2. Concern over a decline in Israel attachment

Much of the current concern with Israel education is driven by the considerable intellectual attention over the past decade that has focused on the "decline" vs. "continuity" debate. Numerous studies report a decline in attachment to Israel, particularly among younger Jews within the American Jewish community (American Jewish Committee, 2003; Cohen, 1998; Cohen & Eisen, 2000; Cohen & Kelman, 2007; Horowitz, 2000; Ukeles et al., 2006). Writing in the October 2010 issue of *Contemporary Jewry*, Sergio DellaPergola summarizes the views of many:

The unequivocal inference from these cross-sectional cohort data is a gradual weakening over time of the relationship of American Jews toward Israel.

Lisa Grant and Ezra Kopelowitz

These [data] point to an unmistakable blurring among the younger of the strong sense of interest, affective involvement, responsibility and caring that American Jewry have historically demonstrated toward the State of Israel and its Jewish community (p.187).

Recently, a counter-voice claims that the "diminishing connection" thesis is wrong. Rather, American Jewry is as attached to Israel as ever and given increased Israel travel and the effect of other factors such as Internet based communication technology we might expect the current generation to develop stronger ties to Israel than their parents (Sasson, Kadushin & Saxe, 2008; Sasson et al., 2010 and 2012).

These exchanges among sociologists and demographers are part of a bustling scene that includes scholarly gatherings, weighty deliberations, market studies, organizational restructurings, and investment of abundant resources and creative capital in an attempt to increase Diaspora Jews' attachment and engagement with Israel.

Alongside the academic and intellectual discourse is the rapidly growing interest in the engagement of Jews with Israel by Jewish Federations, foundations, and the major institutions of Jewish life. The result, organized initiatives to further the attachment of American Jewry to Israel, includes a number of high profile projects such as Birthright Israel and the MASA Israel Journey alongside many other smaller programs. Looking at just one domain, Jewish day schools, we can see major growth of Israel related activity. A recent report on Israel education in Jewish day schools, (Pomson, Dietcher, & Muszkat-Barkan, 2009) counted 40 programs and products (not including curriculum) that are currently offered to high schools to enhance the Israel education they provide. In that same report, the authors estimate that 70% of the non-Orthodox day schools sponsor Israel trips for their students (p. 8).

While much of the focus is currently on high school and college aged students, another arena for increased Israel engagement is the synagogue. In addition to congregational Israel trips, a mainstay for many congregations, a number of community-wide initiatives have focused on creating cultural change that makes Israel a more integral aspect of congregational life by enhancing the quality, frequency, and depth of Israel awareness, education, and engagement. For example, for a number of years the Combined Jewish Philanthropies of Boston conducted a high profile Israel engagement project that focused on local synagogues. Along similar lines, SAJES, the Long Island New York Board of Jewish Education, in partnership with the UJA-Federation of New York, sponsored *Ki Va Mo'ed* an Israel engagement initiative that builds relationships between New York and Israeli congregations.

Yet, even with these redoubled efforts, the data consistently show that in the United States, Jews have a "wide but shallow sympathy for Israel" (Reinharz, 2003, pg. 2). People show their support in times of crisis, but Israel does not figure greatly into religious identity or how most individuals make personal meaning from being Jewish in their everyday life. While there is compelling evidence that American Jewish support for and identification with Israel has remained relatively stable over the last twenty-five years (Sasson et al., 2010 and 2012) there is also a growing discourse that claims that Israel is irrelevant to those who feel fully rooted and at home in America and may be discomfited or alienated from the seeming political morass of contemporary Israeli life (Aviv & Schneer, 2005; Cohen & Kelman, 2007, 2010; Gordis, 2009).

Whether decline or continuity in terms of the numbers, we are sure that in light of the broader trends of religious and communal change occurring in the United States, the quality of the connection that Jews have to Israel is changing. Jews might still be engaged with Israel or not, but the place of Israel (as the place of Jewish community) in their lives will be different, because of the larger changes taking place in American society. A focus on Israel education provides an opportunity to understand these changes from the perspective of work being done by Jewish educators.

The shift in the quality of Jews' orientation to Israel is rooted in a new paradigm emerging for the organization of American Jewish life in general and the connection of American Jews to Israel in particular (Kopelowitz, 2003, 2007; Kopelowitz & Ravid, 2010; Sasson, 2010; Sasson et al., 2010;Wolf & Kopelowitz, 2003). With a focus on the U.S. – Israel relationship, Sasson (2010) argues that since the 1980s, the relationship between Israel and American Jewry has undergone substantial change, shaking up many of the established institutional relationships that govern the field. The change is described in terms of a decline of what Liebman and Cohen first described as a "mass mobilization" paradigm (1990) and the rise of a new paradigm that we refer to as "mutuality and meaning."

Sasson (2010, pp. 174-175) argues:

"The mass mobilization paradigm typified the relationship between American Jews and Israel during the period extending between the early 1950s and the late 1980s....The main tasks of Jewish organizations in relation to Israel were fundraising and political advocacy. Fundraising was organized primarily through the federations as part of the United Jewish Appeal (UJA)...., [D]uring the "mass mobilization" phase, the relationship of American Jewry to Israel was largely centralized, top-down, consensus-oriented, mediated and idealized. American Jews were mobilized by core organizations (UJA, AJC), to donate money to quasi-governmental bodies in Israel (JAFI, Jewish National Fund), and to provide political support for the policies of the government of Israel (i.e., via AIPAC, Conference of Presidents). Travel and immigration were handled largely by the main denominational movements in the United States and the quasi-governmental Jewish Agency for Israel. The mass mobilization of donations and political support encouraged the idealization of Israel but not a direct relationship based on first-hand knowledge or experience".

The way the mass mobilization paradigm plays out in the educational arena is either through Israel advocacy or by using Israel as a way to boost and reinforce Diaspora Jewish identity. While there are many Israel initiatives that are still predicated on this paradigm, we are also seeing a recent wave of Israel initiatives that seek to complement or replace it with educational experiences and approaches that demonstrate how Israel and the Diaspora can enrich each other and as a result, enrich Jewish collective life worldwide. This latter movement is what we refer to as mutuality and meaning.

3. An attempt to reverse failed educational and organizational practices

Educational researchers and thinkers have observed a long-term pattern of Israel education in schools and congregations that both fail to inspire and engage American Jews and fail to make the case that Israel is integral to contemporary American Jewish life (Ackerman, 1996; Chazan 1979, 2005; Grant, 2007). American congregations seem to focus much more on those aspects of Jewish experience that are portable, personal and more immediately relevant to life cycle events, synagogue worship, and holiday rituals. In these experiences (Grant, 2007; Kopelowitz, 2005) Israel is peripheral, something that occurs on an occasional and episodic basis, but hardly a significant feature of the broad educational program. Even among those individuals and institutions at the forefront of programmatic development and innovation, few are able to articulate a clear vision or purpose for teaching Israel that extends beyond the symbolic plane (Pomson et al., 2009).

To sustain a vibrant collective Jewish life, we have to expand the sense of what it means to be part of something larger than the individual. Israel is an essential component of this understanding and experience. We recognize that this is no simple task. There are multiple challenges to engaging Diaspora Jews both in Jewish collective life and with Israel. As individuals, Jews increasingly pick and choose when, where, and how to express themselves Jewishly without drawing upon the rich and integral package of Jewish experiences that encompass religious, cultural, social, and ethnic dimensions. The result is a relatively superficial declaration that "I am Jewish," but one that does not rest on the cultural resources required to turn Judaism into a vital resource for living a rich human life.

Rather than wring our hands in dismay at this attenuation, our task is to find ways to give positive and compelling substance to being a Jew in an open society with porous boundaries. We need to cultivate a deep understanding of what it means to be part of a vibrant Jewish culture. From this perspective, "Israel education" is not a cry of despair against assimilation, but rather a vision for a sustainable and compelling basis for Jewish belonging in an open society; a way of being Jewish and part of the broader world at the same time.

THREE DIMENSIONS OF ISRAEL EDUCATION: "INTEGRATE," "COMPLICATE" AND "CONNECT"

The approach to Israel education that we offer rests on three core principles, from which we derive three educational strategies that we label as "integrate," "complicate," and "connect". Each of the three main sections of this book focus on one of these dimensions which are introduced and defined here.

Principle 1: Integrate - Israel is integral to Judaism and the collective Jewish Experience wherever it is lived.

All too often, Israel is presented and/or represented in an isolated and episodic way through ceremony and celebration, through occasional units of study, and through trips that while powerful experiences, are of limited duration. Though these are all essential components of Israel education, they are insufficient as they perpetuate a bifurcation between Israel and other aspects of Jewish experience. These experiences keep Israel external to core aspects and questions that shape Jewish life and Jewish engagement. Meaningful and enduring Israel education strives to make Israel integral and integrated into Jewish life, not something that happens episodically and ceremonially, but something that occurs routinely and richly. When Israel becomes a regularity of the educational experience, then the ceremonies and symbols take on deeper meaning and relevance in one's life.

Principle 2: Complicate - Israel is a multi-vocal, multi-layered, textured weave that affords the possibility for intellectual, emotional, spiritual, and social engagement with the Land, People, and State of Israel in a way that cultivates a rich sense of belonging and commitment to the Jewish collective.

In today's world, the founding myths of Israel no longer capture the hearts and minds of young Jews in the same way as they did a generation ago. The realities of Israeli politics and culture, the clash between religious and secular Jews, the seemingly endless cycle of violence of the Palestinian-Israeli conflict, and the bitterly contentious views about the occupation (and whether indeed it is an occupation at all) all contribute to an intricate landscape that is difficult to teach, resisted by many educators because they lack the knowledge base to teach it and more importantly perhaps, in their view it threatens to undermine their underlying goal of cultivating love.

This orientation to teaching Israel fits with an advocacy model that presumes you are in "Israel's corner" no matter what. Yet, "to support Israel no matter what," runs counter to one of the core values of liberal education in American society whose goal is to help learners develop the capacity to question, to examine issues from multiple perspectives, and to explore a variety of approaches to analyzing situations and solving problems. Most importantly, it prevents the educator from enabling each student to create a personal connection to Israel that is meaningful and relevant.

When educators and educational institutions encourage independent, critical thinking in other subject areas, but subtly or overtly convey that there is one right way to think about and connect to Israel, they send a mixed message to their students that results in confusion and profound ambivalence towards Israel (Zakai, 2011). Complicating Israel challenges educators to become more comfortable with discomfort, to make the learning more nuanced, multi-layered, and open-ended without asking for or providing clear answers to every question, so that learners can grapple with difficult issues, appreciate diversity and complexity of different points of view, and reflect critically on what it means to them in their own lives. Complicating Israel also challenges educators to relax their stance towards expecting an unreflective love of Israel, and a narrow band of accepted attitudes and behaviors.

Principle 3: Connect - Understanding Israel as a resource for Jewish life establishes a foundation for mutuality among world Jewry.

Recently, we have begun to see a range of initiatives that reject the idea that it is sufficient to simply mobilize individuals on behalf of Israel; instead, initiatives place a strong emphasis on meaningful engagement by individual Diaspora Jews with Israel, in ways that invite serious and substantive interactions, either through: (1) direct person-to-person relationships between Diaspora and Israeli Jews, and/or (2) more meaningful, personalized forms of contact between Diaspora Jews and Israel, based on individuals developing informed opinions about contemporary Israel, including developing a personal philosophy about the major issues of the day in Israel and their implications for Diaspora Jewry.

These forms of connection build on the principle that Jewish life is best experienced in an atmosphere of togetherness. Creating connections with other Jews through time and place, locally and globally is the core practice of Jewish Peoplehood. Creating connections needs to occur both during and after the educational experience. These connections are social, enjoyable, include participation in meaningful ceremonies, and also include conversation and reflection.

With this initial framing in mind, we turn to the core of the book that is organized into four parts plus a conclusion. The first three of these begins by presenting a conceptual framework for the educational dimensions outlined above: integrate, complicate and connect. This overview is followed by a series of vignettes based on our research and extensive observation of the field. The vignettes are designed to illustrate how each of the dimensions comes to life in a variety of Jewish educational settings. Each of the three sections concludes with "notes for educators," these being a discussion of concrete educational strategies.

The fourth section of the book provides a more extensive case study that explores how the integrate, complicate and connect dimensions come together in practice in an actual setting. While the different sections of the book provide a singular focus on each dimension, ultimately, we believe that they need to be seen as interrelated components of an overall strategy for Israel education. The final case study illustrates both the transformative potential and the challenges entailed in this more purposeful approach to Israel education upon which we elaborate further in the conclusion.

I. INTEGRATE: MAKING ISRAEL PART OF ONGOING JEWISH LIFE

Research shows that the more actively Jewish one is the more connected one is to Israel. Levels of attachment to Israel increase as do levels of affiliation and involvement in synagogue life (Ament, 2005; Cohen, 1998; Grant & Kopelowitz, 2009). One reason for this phenomenon is apparent when one walks into most Jewish institutions. Israel is present whether in the posters on a wall, the Israeli flag, the celebration of Israel Independence Day or in other small and large symbols and events that American Jewish institutions mark which in some way connect their constituents to Israel.

A rich Jewish life is by definition an integrative and holistic experience. Excellent Jewish educational institutions reflect that experience. An active Jew is constantly exposed to aesthetic/decorative, ceremonial and conversational dimensions of the Jewish experience, which are captured in the curriculum and broader atmosphere of a Jewish educational organization.

Unfortunately, many educational settings isolate and/or impoverish the Jewish experience at their institutions. Far too often, clear lines of distinction are made between Jewish and secular subjects and formal and informal learning. The result is to create compartmentalized encounters with Jewish culture and knowledge, which are relevant only to the particular educational experience and divorced from the larger life experience in any coherent way.

Israel education as Jewish learning is only relevant to Jewish life to the extent that students break out of a particular ceremony or classroom experience and use the knowledge and skills elsewhere in situations that are part of the larger flow of life. For example, when a school runs an Israel trip, it should not be seen as a separate and isolated experience, but rather as an effort to connect the trip experience to classroom learning and other events taking place at the school. The challenge for an educator who wishes to raise the quality of Israel education is to do so in such a way that Israel is not introduced as a "special topic." If Israel is limited to a one-time course, an "Israel advocacy" seminar, or limited to a trip to Israel, then an individual will regard Israel as just that - "a one time event." There is certainly a place for the academic study of Israel, but this must be seen as part of a broader strategy that infuses Israel into the overall ethos of the educational enterprise.

The successful Israel educational program is "what we do." Excellent Israel education, as with excellent Jewish education, pays attention to the integrative aspects of the Jewish dimension with life. To understand excellence, we look at the lives of active Jews and ask how the acquisition of formal knowledge about Israel and Judaism takes place. We also need to ask how do processes of formal knowledge acquisition intertwine with reading the newspaper, browsing the Internet, participating in ceremonies and the conversations of everyday life? How can Jewish education be systematically organized in Jewish schools to reflect the larger joy of living a rich Jewish life that we see amongst active and committed members of the Jewish community? Israel education is an essential part of this broader discussion.

Israel education at its finest is an integral part of the cultural and educational ethos of a Jewish institution. It might not even appear as a noticeable or perhaps distinct educational strategy; but, rather is woven seamlessly into the daily life of the educational setting. It will include formal and informal opportunities for engagement, learning through academic study, ceremony, conversation and reflection, and experiential learning.

The vignettes in this section and the final case study on Camp Harlam show the multi-dimensional nature of Israel in the life of a Jewish institution. The manner in which Israel integrates is highly contextual depending on the setting and people involved.

The first two vignettes in this section explore how Jewish day schools attempt to seamlessly integrate Israel into their educational fabric. The first takes a macro view by considering how Israel can be integrated into five different dimensions of the educational experience of a Jewish day school. The second vignette takes a micro view exploring how one community day school expresses its commitment to integrating Israel into the school culture through its approach to Hebrew language instruction.

In the third vignette, we look at efforts in four St. Louis synagogues to raise the quality and standard of Israel education by integrating it into more aspects of religious, cultural, and educational life. The vignette describes findings from a research study of four congregations that show how Israel engagement can be employed as a means to both strengthen connections and commitment to Israel and to strengthen the core membership within the community itself.

VIGNETTE 1: FIVE DIMENSIONS
OF ISRAEL IN A JEWISH SCHOOL

What kinds of evidence should we look for in determining where and how Israel is integrated and integral to Jewish educational experiences? This question stood at the heart of a survey of American community Jewish day schools participating in the RAVSAK network[1] (Kopelowitz, 2005).[2] Schools in the RAVSAK network represent a wide variety of Jewish and educational orientations, yet as we will see there are clear patterns to their approach to Israel education. As described in what follows, the survey findings help to illustrate each of these patterns.

In this vignette, which is based on a paper presented at an Israel Education Think Tank held at the Melton Centre of Hebrew University in 2007, we offer an organizing framework for thinking about Israel in a Jewish school in a manageable way. We suggest there are at least five core dimensions to consider in understanding the place of Israel in a Jewish school, each offering a unique conception of time: the (1) aesthetic/ decorative, (2) ceremonial, (3) conversational/ interactive, (4) curricula and the (5) formal management of time. To think strategically about the development of Israel education, we need to first describe each of these and then ask a prescriptive question: How should educators incorporate these five temporal dimensions into an overall strategy for Israel education?

1. Aesthetic and decorative: Constantly in the background

The aesthetic or decorative representation of Israel is one of the most obvious ways to distinguish Jewish settings from secular ones. Almost all Jewish educational settings display Israeli flags, maps and pictures of Israel on bulletin boards and walls. Many Jewish buildings include architectural features that are evocative

---

1 RAVSAK is a member organization designed to support community day schools across North America.
2 Research commissioned by the Jewish Agency for Israel and RAVSAK.

of Israeli landscapes and sites through use of Jerusalem stone, mosaic tiles, Hebrew signage, posters, photographs, or other media. One might also hear Israeli music when placed on hold on the telephone or over the intercom system, see Israeli newspapers in the library, or even hear broadcasts of Israeli television or radio amongst other possible examples.

Israel's constant appearance as an aesthetic or decorative presence may be perceived as "simply always there," in a seen but often unnoticed fashion. The question is less about the presence of Israel but rather the intensity of the use of "Israel as background." For example: Where do Israeli flags and maps appear? Are they in public spaces for all to see, or in the more intimate and private spaces of classrooms?

By looking at the placement of the Israeli flag as a symbol used to mark a school as a Jewish space, we learn that there is a difference between presentations of Jewishness to those who enter the school, as opposed to the presentation of the school as a Jewish institution vis-à-vis the outside world. This is made apparent by the fact that while 74% of the schools in the RAVSAK survey reported feeling comfortable hanging the Israeli flag in their classrooms, only 29% are willing to make a similar statement of Israel as a symbolic marker of the schools Jewishness vis-à-vis the outside world, by flying the flag in front of their building.

The map of Israel has less of a presence than the Israeli flag in these RAVSAK schools, though it is also a dominant force. Maps are hung by 69% of the schools only in their Jewish studies classrooms. Thirty percent hang a map of Israel in every classroom in their school.

2. Ceremony: A cyclical experience of time

In contrast to the continuous or constant presence of Israel as a decorative or aesthetic dimension of life in a Jewish school, ceremony is episodic. Ceremonies mark distinct periods of time that can last from brief moments to several days. What they share is that in ceremonial experiences, people step out of the routine experience of everyday life and enter into a different "communal" sense of reality. The most prominent example is the celebration of Israel Independence Day. In the RAVSAK survey, 100% of schools reported holding an Israel Independence Day ceremony. For a few hours once a year the school community leaves aside regular classroom learning and shares a common ceremonial experience that connects them as a community to Israel. In some schools the Israel Independence Day ceremony also serves as a springboard for a larger integrative experience where additional classroom learning and other informal educational activities are devoted to Israel prior to and after the ceremony. It may also result in a more intensive aesthetic/decorative presence through the display of flags, maps, pictures, and other artifacts.

The key aspect of the ceremony is its cyclical nature. The ceremony occurs at regular and expected intervals. It is a moment out of everyday routine, which is taken for granted in the sense that people expect it to happen, but normally requires tremendous work and preparation for successful execution. In a successful ceremony, participants step outside of their everyday identity and experience a transcendent feeling that celebrates a particular aspect of Jewish life and culture that is shared with other Jews the world over.

RAVSAK schools participate in other ceremonial activities directly related to Israel in a cultural, nationalist or religious sense to varying degrees. In the survey, 70% of schools reported commemorating *Yom HaZikaron* (Remembrance Day for Israel's fallen soldiers), 65% hold a *Tu Beshvat seder* and 30% participate in an annual Israel Day parade. 100% of schools also reported that there are special occasions when their students sing *Hatikvah,* the Israeli national anthem. Fully 45% of the schools report that the Israeli national anthem is sung daily, though the majority limits the singing of *Hatikvah* to school wide assemblies.

While not often categorized as such, a school-sponsored Israel trip can also be seen as a type of ceremony (Kopelowitz, Wolf, &

Markowitz, 2009; Pomson et al., 2009). Like the Israel Independence Day celebration, the Israel trip can also serve as an integrative force pulling together different aspects of the Israel experience at the school into a larger educational experience.

3. Conversation and interaction: An unstable experience of time

A third, less common dimension in which Israel might be experienced in a Jewish school is through conversation and interactive social activities. The key difference between a ceremony and a conversation is that the latter is unpredictable and dynamic. Whereas in a ceremony, interaction is scripted and all know their role, in a conversation or open-ended interaction participants are never quite sure what will occur.

In contrast to the aesthetic/decorative and ceremonial experiences of Israel that are regular in either a constant or cyclical sense, conversation represents an unstable experience that is closer to the experience of everyday life as it is actually lived outside of school. The individual needs to develop a sense of self to successfully participate in a conversation – to develop an opinion or set of skills that can be applied to help the conversation move forward. The test of an individual's opinion or skills is immediately felt in the reaction of others – "are they impressed? Do they offer a counter opinion, or do they simply dismiss the credibility of what I just said?"

The RAVSAK survey touched on the extent to which Israel is discussed in the classroom in an open-ended fashion that allows students to form independent opinions and put them to the conversational test. Here, 47% of schools reported encouraging their students to participate in programs that enable a connection to students in an Israeli school or to Israeli youth in general. The question of course is about the quality, intensity, and content of the interaction between the American and Israeli students in these programs. For example, if a school sponsors a video-conference with an Israeli school is there an opportunity for debate and argument, or does it remain on the symbolic level as a polite ceremony in which teachers maintain strict control over the event? Likewise, on an Israel trip is there time for students to interact with their Israeli peers in educational situations that allow for significant exchanges of opinions and opportunities for peer-learning; or, do they spend their time site-seeing but never entering into significant debate that brings each student to critically examine his or her personal connection to Israel?

4. Curriculum – a linear or cumulative experience of time

Within the school, knowledge and experience is often compartmentalized into disciplines with a curriculum for in-class and out of class education that will ensure the accumulation of knowledge and skills needed to master a particular discipline. In this sense, Israel is like math or science. A curriculum assumes a linear or cumulative experience of time. If the curriculum for a particular discipline is followed, each semester represents progress. A student becomes more knowledgeable and able in the areas germane to the particular discipline.

The following table represents an attempt made in the RAVSAK survey to understand how Israel-related topics fit into the formal educational curriculum of the responding schools. The table shows Israel-related topics that might be taught in a community day school and their standing vis-à-vis general Jewish topics in theory ("what should be taught") and in practice ("what is actually taught"). The results show that Israel through the teaching of Hebrew and history receives an honorable place in the educational curricula of RAVSAK affiliated day schools. These two areas are both regarded as high priority and taught in practice. In comparison, areas touching on contemporary Israeli society are regarded as lower priority and even lower in terms of topics actually taught.

The Ideal vs. Real in the School Curriculum

Ideal: In your opinion, how much importance should a Jewish community school attach to each of the following subjects?

Real: In the previous question we asked about the ideal position of each subject in a communities school's curriculum. What in fact is the actual importance of each of the following subjects within your school's curriculum?

Possible Answers: "not important at all" (score = 1), "somewhat important" (score = 2), "important" (score = 3) and "very important" (score = 4).

Orientation	Subject	Ideal	Real	Gap
Culture/Israel	Hebrew Language	4.0	3.9	0.1
Religion	Tanakh	3.9	3.7	0.1
Israel	History of State of Israel	3.8	3.4	0.5
Religion	Prayer	3.7	3.7	0.1
History	The Holocaust	3.5	3.3	0.3
History	World Jewish History	3.5	2.9	0.6
Israel	Israeli Culture	3.4	3.0	0.4
Israel	Israel-Diaspora Relations	3.3	2.7	0.7
History	American Jewish History	3.3	2.8	0.5
Israel	Geography of State of Israel	3.3	2.9	0.4
Israel	Israel in Jewish Sources	3.2	2.4	0.8
Israel	Israel/Palestinian Conflict	3.2	2.5	0.7
Israel	Hebrew Literature	3.0	2.7	0.3
Current Events	Central Issues American/Canadian Society	2.9	2.1	0.7
Religion	Mishnah	2.8	2.0	0.8
Current Events/Israel	Central Issues Israeli Society	2.6	2.1	0.6
Religion	Gemara	2.6	1.8	0.8

For the purposes of this discussion, the specific topics to cover in an Israel education curriculum are less important than how the development of curriculum might be integrated with the constant, cyclical and episodic conceptions of time that are present in the other three dimensions of Israel education discussed above. The secret to success in Jewish education is to bring all four conceptions of time into a coherent whole, where each complements and strengthens the other.

One example, given above, is the class trip to Israel. The trip is first and foremost a pilgrimage ceremony. Students and teachers leave their everyday world and venture forth as a group to the religious, national, and cultural center of the Jewish People. During this time away, the Jewish group dimension becomes central and integrative in a manner that is almost impossible to achieve in a regular school day when the majority of time is given over to math, science, sports and other secular subjects.

However, the successful school trip will also include non-ceremonial aspects, such as time for debate and argument, developing personal relationships with Israeli peers, and studying topics that reinforce and expand upon classroom learning at school prior to the trip and which will continue after the trip. Finally, pictures and other material artifacts related to the trip become part of the aesthetic/decorative environment back at school.

5. Organizational management of time

The reality is that integration of all four Israel dimensions into a coherent whole is the exception, rather than the norm in Jewish schools. One reason has to do with how time is managed and allocated. To integrate the different dimensions of Israel into the overall economy of time within the school requires a tremendous investment of thought and attention. In contrast, the easiest and most traveled path is to divide and conquer. Each discipline is developed independently of the others in the school. Each ceremony has a team who is responsible for design and implementation. Each school trip is taken as an event unto itself. No one need raise their head to look beyond their immediate responsibility and examine the contribution of the particular activity to the school's larger Jewish mission.

In order to integrate the different dimensions of Israel, time must be taken out of the otherwise busy staff schedule for the express purpose of getting people who specialize in a particular area to open themselves up to the work of others. For this to happen, the head of school and in many cases the board also must back the initiative. Time equals money. Without necessary resources the larger commitment to producing an integrated Jewish experience at the school, of which Israel is a part, will not happen.

While we are unaware of any academic work that documents the manner in which the different dimensions of Israel education is integrated at a school, the educational work done by a small number of schools that come close to the ideal, serves as a good example for how this might occur. For example there are schools that encourage their Hebrew and Jewish studies teachers to work together to plan the school's Israel trip and to organize the Israel Independence Day ceremony. In contrast, in most schools the Hebrew teachers (i.e., the Israelis) are responsible for all planning that directly related to Israel. The result is a practical and conceptual divide between the Israeli teachers who come to represent "Israel" and Jewish studies teachers whose work represents the narrowly defined "Jewish" aspects of the schools' educational work. By bringing the teachers to work together, the hope is that Jewish studies and Israel education will become one. The next step in such a process would be to bring secular studies (math, languages, science, art, etc.) teachers into the conversation.

In conclusion, for Israel to become a significant part of the life of a school, and the life of its students, time must be put aside to work through the points at which Israel turns into a resource for enriching the broader educational experience.

VIGNETTE 2: JCDS – INTEGRATING ISRAEL THROUGH HEBREW

Integrating Israel into the life of a Jewish day school could be seen as one of the core responsibilities of the Hebrew department. However, when Hebrew is treated as subject alongside math, English, history, Bible and the like, this can lead more to compartmentalization than integration. Where Hebrew is more integral to the curriculum, and can be heard in the hallways, on the loudspeakers, and in classrooms throughout the day, the language and culture of Israel become more natural parts of the ambiance and content of daily life in school.

Such is the case at the Jewish Community Day School (JCDS), a community day school just outside of Boston, Massachusetts. This vignette is based on a multi-year evaluation study of JCDS' Hebrew program.[3] JCDS has about 180 students in kindergarten through 8th grade. The school's vision and mission articulates five core commitments: Hebrew language, Israel, religious pluralism, curricular integration, and child-centered instruction. All of these commitments contribute to the significant presence of Israel at this school in all five dimensions as described in the preceding vignette. The school leadership, both lay and professional, sees Hebrew as means to a greater end of helping reflect the place of Hebrew and Israel in their vision for Jewish life. As Sharona Givol, the Hebrew coordinator stated: "At JCDS, language instruction is more than language instruction - it is an induction into Israeli life and culture, including history, geography, social issues and so on."

JCDS attempts to fully integrate Hebrew across the curriculum and throughout the day. They strive to make Hebrew not a second language but instead a natural and integral part of the Jewish life and culture of the school.

---

3 Research commissioned by The Covenant Foundation.

While Hebrew language has long been a priority at the school, the school adopted the Proficiency Approach to Hebrew instruction starting in 2003, under the guidance of Vardit Ringwald, professor of Hebrew at Brandeis University and through the support of a five-year grant from the Covenant Foundation. This recognized methodology is considered to be the "industry standard" in foreign language instruction by the American Council on the Teaching of Foreign Languages (ACTFL). The approach is a child-centered, constructivist methodology that requires personalization and customization of the curriculum to fit with the interests and motivations of the teacher and the learners. In other words, there is no prepared curriculum; rather, the curriculum is developed by the teachers who choose topics based on their interests and what they perceive to be relevant to the students' lives. This requires teachers who are both rigorously trained in the methodology, and who are wholly sensitive to the needs and developmental capabilities of their learners. Progress is made possible through the constant support of a mentor who is fully present in the daily lives of the teachers and students at the school.

The Hebrew curriculum utilizes materials that are written or produced by a native speaker for a native speaker. Thus, the school strives to convey Israeli culture naturally through the language. Students engage in learning Hebrew by singing Israeli songs, watching Israeli television or movies, reading poems and stories, learning dances, playing games, and having conversations in Hebrew about their own lives through the various activities in which they engage.

The Proficiency Approach gives equal attention to developing reading and speaking skills through conversation, drill, and examination. A detailed process of student assessment includes the Oral Proficiency Interview (OPI), a standardized and carefully structured conversation between a trained and certified interviewer and the student. The OPI measures how well students speak a language by comparing their performance of specific language tasks with the criteria for each of ten proficiency levels established by the ACTFL. By 2007, four years after introducing the Proficiency Approach, 73% of students at JCDS met these established expectations. The great majority of these students were at the Intermediate Level. Most of those who remained at the Novice Level were students with learning disabilities and most of those at the Advanced Level were heritage learners, having one or more native Hebrew-speaking parent.

As noted, the Proficiency Approach relies heavily on regular and ongoing mentoring and professional development of teachers who are both trained in the instructional methods and ultimately become curriculum writers. The school has a full-time Hebrew coordinator who develops instructional resources, provides extensive support and ongoing professional development with the faculty. She also conducts student assessments of proficiency benchmarks. In addition to the classroom Hebrew teachers, there is also a full-time Hebrew Resource Teacher who works with students who have special needs, both in the classroom and on a one-to-one basis, as needed.

During multiple visits over several years, it was clear to see that Hebrew is omnipresent at JCDS. Virtually every hallway display showed student work in Hebrew, or was focused on Israel, or both. Hebrew is literally on the lips of students and faculty throughout the day. For example, the school has a "young ambassador" program where 7th grade volunteers take visitors through the school on a guided tour in Hebrew. Hebrew can be heard in the teachers' room and in exchanges between teachers and between teachers and students. Hebrew is not only taught in Hebrew classes, but is often the language used in art, music, and drama electives.

Multiple classroom observations included those where new materials were introduced, those that focused primarily on review and reinforcement of material already learned, and those that focused on application of material already learned to new contexts. With very minor exceptions for word clarifications, the teachers provided all their instructions and comments in Hebrew. In the more advanced classes, the students spoke almost entirely in Hebrew. English was more present in the novice classes, but even there, the students seemed engaged with the process and motivated to find the vocabulary to express themselves in Hebrew. When they hesitated or stumbled, the teacher would gently remind them of the word and they would go on, without any apparent embarrassment.

The observation team saw many instances where students had the opportunity to use Hebrew in "natural" conversation, such as sharing what they did after school the day before, talking about their summer vacation plans, and even telling the guest what they were learning. We saw many instances where students helped each other, reminding them of words, and politely correcting each other. We even heard students complain about learning Hebrew in different classes. All of this suggests that a positive learning environment has been created for Hebrew at JCDS.

The impetus for this strong commitment and engagement with Hebrew and Israeli culture comes both from the school leadership and the parents. The administrative leaders of the school see the approach to Hebrew as a critical educational and social value in their learning community and are enthusiastic about teacher satisfaction and student progress. Parents are likewise extremely supportive of the intensive focus on Hebrew at the school. In 2008, a survey administered to parents showed that 50% of homes have at least one parent who speaks Hebrew (though is not necessarily a native Hebrew speaker). A similar percentage of respondents said that they socialize frequently or very frequently with Hebrew speakers, suggesting a very high level of engagement with Israel and Israeli culture. More than three-quarters of the parents responding expressed a very high desire for their children to become fluent in modern Hebrew both to help improve their text study skills and to connect them to Israel.

The parents and educators of the JCDS appear to be a community at the highly committed and connected end of the Israel engagement spectrum. The school leadership states that the integration of Israel into the school through Hebrew language and the use of authentic materials is such an obvious expression of their commitment to Israel that it's "*muvan me'eilav*" – it goes without saying. Their success with students' proficiency is carefully documented. Their culture seems richly infused with Israel as a natural and integral part of Jewish life both within and beyond the school. This is evident in virtually every dimension of daily school life as described in the first vignette of this section. Hebrew as a means to express and explore Israeli culture is woven throughout the school, through symbol and ceremony, through the use of "authentic" curricular materials such as Israeli film, music and literature, and through the organic use of Hebrew "throughout the day" – in announcements, informal conversations between faculty and between faculty and students. This makes JCDS a model worthy of emulation for other schools considering how to take richer advantage of Hebrew language instruction as a vehicle for cultural infusion and making Israel a more natural part of Jewish identity development.

VIGNETTE 3: BUILDING LEADERSHIP FOR ENGAGEMENT WITH ISRAEL IN SYNAGOGUES

While much communal attention to Israel engagement focuses on the high school and college arenas, considerable related work is taking place with synagogues as well. Such initiatives are often undertaken through the sponsorship of the local Jewish Federation and typically involve several synagogues within the community.

Synagogues are the central institution for Jewish engagement in North American Jewish life. Just as in Jewish schools and other Jewish educational settings, the nature of Israel engagement varies widely depending on a host of factors. Professional and lay leadership are key to setting the tone and communicating the place of Israel in the life of the congregation. However, there are also varying degrees of engagement amongst the congregants themselves that suggest a singular approach to Israel may be overly simplistic and ultimately ineffective.

This vignette presents a way of thinking about and understanding how to integrate Israel into multiple dimensions of congregational life. It builds on research that suggests that the greatest potential for engaging congregants with Israel rests with those who are among the committed core of congregational life. The research is drawn from an initiative called *Knesset Israel* (KI) that was sponsored by the St. Louis Federation. KI began in 2008 and involved four synagogues in St. Louis, three Reform and one Conservative. The overarching goal for *Knesset Israel* was: "To re-imagine Israel in our congregations." Research conducted for the KI project provides a rich understanding of how Israel might integrate into and strengthen synagogue life, or the life of other Jewish organizations that strive to deepen the connection of their constituents to Israel. The research included interviews with the leadership teams in the four participating synagogues and an Internet based survey of members of those synagogues conducted between January and February 2009, at approximately the halfway point of the larger initiative.

Knesset Israel

Knesset Israel (KI) was the synagogue component of a larger initiative called Focus Israel, a joint project of the St. Louis Federation and MAKOM, the Israel engagement network of the Jewish Agency for Israel (JAFI). Participants in Focus Israel included area rabbis, executive directors, Jewish educators, and lay board presidents of Jewish agencies and congregations. The goal was to create cultural change that would place Israel more centrally in the hearts and minds of the St. Louis Jewish community through strategic programming, advocacy, and education.

In the first year of KI, the leadership teams from each congregation worked to create a strategic plan for working with their congregations. Each leadership team included a senior rabbi, senior educator, one lay leader, and a combination (depending on the team) of an early childhood director, teen programmer, additional lay people or synagogue professionals. This planning year included regular learning sessions with nationally recognized scholars, team meetings, a 10-day seminar in Israel, and a post Israel seminar retreat.

The goal of the research was to better understand the impact of KI in each congregation through the end of its first year, and to offer strategic advice, based on survey data, for the best path forward to implement KI's goals. The research was conducted approximately one year into the two-year process and was framed around two key questions:

1. How do different groups within the participating synagogues relate to Israel in their personal lives and in the context of the synagogues?

2. What are the implications for KI in terms of Israel engagement work with each of these groups?

The KI leadership articulated the following four goals during their interviews.

Goal One: Engaging with Israel as an integrated process

To varying degrees, respondents from all four congregations spoke about their vision for Israel engagement as an integrated process, not something episodic and separate from other aspects of Jewish life. For two of the synagogues' leadership teams, the focus was on education, developing "something systemic" that needs to begin in pre-school and continue through a post-confirmation trip, and then more adult education. One rabbi said:

Our leadership needs to be involved and excited about Israel. It should be a basic part of everything we do, just like we always light candles on Friday night, there always should be a natural integrated role for Israel in everything we do.

Similarly, another rabbi focused on Israel as a connective thread that "transcends religion, culture, politics – goes way beyond all of those things."

Goal Two: Enabling individuals to engage in critical discussion

At two of the synagogues, the rabbis noted their political leanings and how this shapes their vision for an Israel engaged congregation that has taken off the "rose colored glasses" in their understanding of Israel. One rabbi stated:

A lot of people who have that deep love of Israel purposefully let themselves be blinded to ways that Israel can improve; that turns off others. My goals for our large and diverse community are to blend that and share the fervent love and also be able to share discussions about what needs to improve.

Another rabbi expressed similar sentiments:

Having a center-left rabbi who raises human rights issues, talks about what it means to be occupiers – that sensitivity has begun to prompt younger and not only younger members to begin to think and read in areas they haven't thought about before. That's an important part of the transition – our ability to engage with the real Israel. Real is the wrong word – what Israel could/should be. Why is there a Jewish People? What do we stand for? What does our life need to look like in a place that's sovereign to us?

A third rabbi focused on the importance of helping "people realize that it is ok to criticize Israel…there are serious conflicts and we aren't always on the right side".

Goal Three: Strengthening People-to-People Connections

Respondents at all four congregations spoke about strengthening People-to-People connections between their congregants and Israelis. They gave a variety of specific examples for how this might be accomplished. All mentioned their desire to bring in Israeli *shlichim* (emissaries) to work in their formal and informal educational programs. Two congregations saw this work as being best accomplished through strengthening ties with their sister congregations in Israel. Respondents from a third congregation mentioned hiring a second rabbi who is a graduate of Machon Schechter (the Conservative Movement's Rabbinical Seminary in Israel), and buying a congregational apartment in Israel for use by members when they visit.

Goal Four: Community Collaboration

While not directly related to Israel engagement, respondents at all four congregations also uniformly spoke in positive terms about the value of community collaboration as part of the KI process. Most talked about how collaborating on KI has broken down some of the competitive nature of St. Louis congregations through sharing of ideas and resources, especially with regard to bringing in scholars and artists from outside the local community. Most also spoke about how collaboration generates more ideas, more good will, more energy, and promotes a feeling of a common bond between the Jewish People. Thus, the very fact of working together across institutional lines within a community seems to be one way to build a stronger consciousness of a connection to the Jewish collective.

Mapping congregant approaches to Israel engagement

Knesset Israel was a change initiative designed to utilize Israel engagement as a means for enriching the Jewish lives of congregants and for Jewish community development. The question faced by the KI leadership at the time of the research was how to attain this broad goal?

Analysis of the survey data led the researchers to suggest a strategy whereby congregational professionals and lay leaders think of Israel engagement as part of a larger process of involvement in congregational life. Success depends on Israel becoming an "obvious" resource for facilitating personal identity development and involvement in Jewish life. The implementation of such a strategy requires a fine-grained understanding of the Jewish needs and motivations of different groups within a congregation, and the manner in which, due to their needs and motivations, congregants will seek to use Israel engagement as a resource for enriching their Jewish lives.

Survey respondents reported on the nature of their involvement in congregational life, their motivations for participating in Jewish life and where Israel fits into their general Jewish needs. In addition respondents were asked for their understanding of the place of Israel in congregational life. The analysis of survey data let to a series of recommendations for how the KI leadership teams can best use Israel as a platform for community development vis-à-vis each of the groups.

Respondents' answers to survey questions about participation in congregational sponsored events and activities, revealed two clear patterns of congregational involvement and engagement with Israel.

1. Highly involved – Committed to Jewish pursuits, but with room to increase the place of Israel in their lives.

Members of the highly involved group, especially those with children, are either maintaining or intensifying their involvement in congregational life. These highly involved respondents are seeking out intensive interaction with Jewish community including their own educational enrichment and that of their children. However, the survey data showed that even for the highly involved, "strengthening a connection to Israel" is a low priority relative to their other Jewish needs. While relative to the uninvolved congregants, Israel is still a strong Jewish need for the involved, it appears that much more can be done to move Israel up to a higher place in their lives; with significant results for the quality of overall involvement in their congregational community.

2. Low involved – Primarily involved for and through their children

The uninvolved group seeks involvement with the congregational community primarily for their children's education. Once their children are grown, the uninvolved are the most likely group to decrease their involvement in congregational life. In general, the uninvolved express fewer strong Jewish needs on which KI can build. They are also less likely than the involved to make a connection between their Jewish needs and Israel engagement. The major Jewish need expressed by the uninvolved is to celebrate Jewish holidays with their families and to connect to Jewish community.

An effective strategy – First empower highly involved congregants to more deeply engage with Israel and then reach out to others

For the KI leadership teams, getting uninvolved congregants excited about Israel engagement is an unrealistic challenge in the short-term. Like those who are involved, "strengthening their connection to Israel" is at the bottom of uninvolved congregants' list of Jewish needs. However, three times as many (36%) of the involved congregants rate connecting to Israel as a strong Jewish need (1.9 on a scale of 1= "to a great extent" and 4 = "not at all"), compared to only 12% of the uninvolved (8% of the uninvolved with children) who say "strengthening their connection to Israel" is a strong Jewish need. Thus, the involved congregants appear to be a far more fertile group to focus on in the early stages of the KI process.

Programming topics or themes

The survey data reveals areas of congregational life where there is significant interest in more Israel engagement among highly involved congregants. These include young adult programming, religious school, adult education, Brotherhood, Sisterhood, and early childhood programs. These domains include opportunities for formal education, cultural and social events, and family programs, virtually the full gamut of congregational offerings. Programming in these areas needs to be sensitive to generational differences about the place of Israel in people's lives, and the difference between families with and without children at home.

Having compelling data to direct the change process is essential but does not guarantee success. As research on other synagogue change processes has made abundantly clear, implementing change is a complex and long-term endeavor (Aron et al., 2010; Reimer, 1997, Wertheimer, 2009). However, using the data to make strategic decisions about where to focus the change initiatives should contribute greatly to the potential for success. For instance, one common assumption shared by many clergy and educators is to look to worship and life cycle events as places to integrate more Israel-related content, especially since these are where Jews "show up" in the congregation. However, the findings from this research show that even involved congregants are not clamoring for Israel to have a greater role in these areas. Focusing efforts here may build resistance and undermine the overall initiative towards integration. In contrast, any programming that contributes to the ability of families to celebrate holidays together and build a connection to community will be well received. Integrating Israel education into these areas of Jewish communal involvement will provide the entry points for engaging congregants in areas such as debate, discussion and People-to-People connections.

The data also reveal the challenge of meeting goals such as developing a more nuanced, critical engagement of congregants with Israel and encouraging congregants to establish interpersonal connections with Israeli Jews. These two strategies are largely driven by professional desires and are not yet high priorities for most congregants. Here is where a strategy, which focuses attention on the highly involved members comes into play; as these are the individuals who are most open to learning about, engaging with, and seeking meaning from a richer relationship with Israel and her People.

The move towards emphasizing robust and meaningful Israel engagement is certainly gathering steam among the leadership of the American Jewish community. What is already clear is that in order to increase the chance of success and most effectively use the resources allocated to the effort, research is vital. While accumulated experience will point practitioners and policy makers towards solutions, without systematic empirical research the learning process is likely to be haphazard and will take much longer to reach a sophisticated understanding of where to focus Israel engagement efforts and what processes are in fact working.

Places to begin

Building a robust engagement with Israel in American congregations is a process similar to other initiatives that seek to transform congregations into richer learning and worship communities. In general and with regard to Israel engagement in particular, readiness for change depends on a number of key factors. Most important it requires a core group of dedicated lay leaders and professionals with the motivation to push change forward (Aron, 2000). Change is most likely to occur when dissatisfaction with the status quo is greater than the perceived cost of the change. Change happens when people want it and there is a leadership group who will make it happen. Yet, dissatisfaction and leadership alone cannot guarantee a successful change process. Those championing the change must have a clear vision for an improved future and concrete ideas as to how to begin the process (Aron et al., 2010).

The KI initiative appears to have met the readiness requirement by assembling leadership teams and garnering their commitment to proceed with a mode of Israel engagement integrated into the Jewish life of their congregations. This mode of Israel engagement embraces complex issues and fosters opportunities for more personal connections with both Israel and Israelis. The research helped to identify four key goals that if implemented provide a framework for developing vision: 1) Integrating Israel into core systems and experiences of a congregation's Jewish life; 2) Engaging in critical conversations about Israel; 3) Strengthening People-to-People connections; and 4) Enhancing community collaboration through Israel programming and the KI process.

This study of Knesset Israel provides solid data that identifies where and among which congregants the desire for change is greatest and where it is the least. These findings can help the congregational teams refine their vision and shape how and where they target their efforts for specific constituents and in specific areas of synagogue life where congregants and professionals want to see a greater Israel presence. Starting points are those areas where highly involved congregations are most likely to want more intensive conversations about the place of Israel in their congregation and congregants' lives. Ultimately, for KI to succeed the leadership teams need to expand the circle of enthusiasts who will not only attend KI programming but also help push it forward at each congregation.

VIGNETTE 4: ISRAEL TRAVEL – ON THE NEED FOR FOLLOW-UP STRATEGIES

Thus far the vignettes in this section focus on multiple ways that Israel integrates into the space of a school or synagogue, and the need to consider different populations and their connection to Jewish life and Israel. As we learned in the first vignette, there is also a temporal dimension to the connection between points of time so that an educational experience is not an isolated event, disconnected from core practices, experiences and ideas that inform an individual's life and the educational environment.

Often Jewish educational programs are deemed successful if they effectively engage participants in some aspect of Jewish life. Engagement, however, by definition, is in "the here and now". By design, engagement experiences are intensive and emotional. Often, they are peak experiences that on first blush may be reported as "life-changing" but in reality, once participants come down from the peak, life resumes as usual.

"The Israel Experience" epitomizes this dilemma. It is a central and perhaps the most developed area of Israel education, but often stands in isolation from participants' lives back home. Since the founding of the State of Israel, educational institutions have organized trips for Diaspora youth to Israel. In the early years these were limited to small groups, primarily youth movement leaders. However, over time, the trip to Israel has reached large segments of the organized Jewish community. These include youth trips that range from one week to one year and sometimes longer for participants as young as 8th grade to post-college graduates. Trip organizers cover the entire ideological spectrum of Diaspora Jewish life. Within the modern Orthodox community, a year in Israel between high school and college is a standard rite of passage. At present, tens of thousands participate in Birthright Israel each year, with many thousands more coming on high school, camp, and youth movement trips as well as programs aimed at college students and post-college young adults (Kopelowitz et al., 2009).[4]

On the one hand, there is tremendous professional knowledge about how to run Israel educational programs. Evaluators in the field today are able to distinguish between that which is excellent and that which is not. On the other hand, one area remains about which we know little, namely the post-trip experience. This vignette presents an argument for the importance of post-trip follow-up to shift the Israel Experience from an episodic and largely ceremonial trip to a more integral aspect of Jewish identity development and Jewish life. This integrative approach, we argue, will have a significant role in ensuring a long-term impact of Israel educational travel programs.

While there is a wide range of program types, based on length, program provider, ideology and the like, overall, Israel Experience programs share basic goals as articulated by the late Shlomo Gravetz, former head of the Youth and HeChalutz (Pioneer) Department of the World Zionist Organization:

In the age of free choice of identity, one meaningful tool, perhaps the most meaningful, for linking the individual Jew with the collective Jewish fate is the bond with the Land of Israel, the State of Israel and Israel society. The Israel Experience is an educational tool, a hands-on experience, aimed first and foremost at bringing individuals closer to the historic heritage, which has Israel as its centre, and in this way to tie them to Judaism, to Israel and to Zionism. The minimum that the program must achieve is the involvement of the young people in the community in which they live (Cohen, 2008, p. 8-9).

In the statement by Gravetz, the following elements appear:

1.   Jewish belonging as a choice made by individuals.

2.   The Israel trip as important resource or "educational tool" for helping young Jews in the formative stages of

---

4 Prominent publications on the Israel Experience include Chazan, 1994; Cohen, 2008; Cohen & Wall, 1994; Kelner, 2002, 2010; Saxe & Chazan, 2008.

their lives connect to the Jewish People and Judaism by way of the Israel Experience.

3. Increased personal involvement of the participant with Israel.

4. Increased involvement of the participant with Jewish life in their home community after trip.

These four points remain central; but to date, research has focused only on the first three; the reasons why individuals choose to travel to Israel, the travel experience, the educational program and the immediate impact on participants. Little research exists about Gravetz's fourth point - the long-term influence of the Israel trip in terms of the manner in which the travel experience integrates back into the life of the participant after returning home. What, if any, influence does an Israel educational trip have on engagement with Jewish life and/or one's sense of Jewish belonging over the long term?

The following case study indicates that the answer to the question of long term impact of an Israel trip is: "very little;" that is, unless there is an organized form of post-trip follow-up.

Case Study: Post Birthright

Birthright Israel (BRI) is the largest venue for bringing young adult Jews to Israel. Most importantly, BRI successfully targets people who have not previously been on an educational trip to Israel. Families who send their children to Israel in high school are more likely than the family of the average BRI participant to have a strong affiliation with the organized Jewish community.

BRI has sponsored extensive research on the quality and impact of the BRI trips since its inception in 1999; however, only recently has the organization begun to pay attention to what happens after the trip. That research shows an impact on a participants' cognitive and emotional connection to Israel, but relatively low levels of increased Jewish communal involvement after BRI participants graduate college (Chertok, Sasson & Saxe, 2009).

Our findings suggest that years later most alumni continue to view Taglit as a watershed experience. It catalyzed their personal connection to the Jewish people, Israel, and their own Jewish identity. However, as post-college age young adults, they remain "tourists" in the Jewish communal world, sightseeing at a few programs but, overall, struggling to find ways to connect. Moreover, given their developmental stage of life, modest Jewish experiential background, and limited knowledge, most alumni are not yet ready to become full-fledged "citizens" of their Jewish communities (Chertok, Sasson & Saxe, 2009, p. 2).

BRI is trying to address this issue through the development of Birthright Next, which focuses on post-trip follow-up.

BRI is without doubt a powerful collective Jewish experience that successfully engages its participants. It is structured to capture the mind and soul, but without intensive educational work, will not typically produce long-term change. As such, it does not generate "Peoplehood consciousness" (Grant & Ravid, 2011; Kopelowitz & Ravid, 2009), which is a much more multi-layered endeavor that includes developing both an emotional and intellectual connection to the idea and reality of the Jewish People and practical contexts for Jews to act on behalf of or as part of the Jewish collective.

The cognitive and emotional engagement that is triggered by successful Israel travel experiences is a necessary but insufficient pre-condition to further engagement with Jewish life. The Israel trip sparks interest and excitement, but the internalization of values, beliefs, and the ability to act on them requires a different kind of educational intervention. If the Israel experience exists outside of a participant's "life's routine" (Kelner, 2010), then a critical step enabling participants to internalize the experience is missed. Focusing on developing a Peoplehood consciousness entails deeper and ongoing forms of teaching and commitment. It requires educational organizations to create ongoing resources and opportunities for living as a Jewishly informed life in an on-going manner.

The following are two examples of how focused post-trip programming leads to increased Jewish involvement by BRI participants.

1. Engagement of educators with BRI participants immediately before, during and after the trip.

In 2008, Hillel: The Foundation for Campus Jewish Life (Hillel) began to place full-time professional Jewish educators on college campuses in the United States. These "Senior Jewish Educators" (SJEs) are largely freed of other responsibilities to the campus Hillel operation. They focus on encouraging students to engage in meaningful Jewish experiences.

Research conducted for Hillel (Cohen et al., 2010) shows the SJEs intentionally seek out interaction with students either before or after the BRI trip. Surveys of students on SJE campuses showed that BRI participants who meet with an SJE exhibit far greater growth in their participation in Jewish life on campus than those who do not. *Without an SJE involved, BRI shows no impact on participants compared to those who didn't go on BRI.*

Earlier research suggests that the opportunity to engage in a post-trip conversation with a knowledgeable mentor can help people articulate, clarify and make deeper meaning out of their feelings and experiences in Israel (Grant, 2001). Interviews with the students confirm that conversations with the SJE fulfill a similar role. A student who experiences a powerful meaningful Jewish experience on BRI has an avenue to further explore and process the experience through conversation with their SJEs. The SJE also recommends and encourages increased Jewish involvement after the trip.

On some Hillel campuses, there are student interns who participate in a year-long leadership development and Jewish learning program, and who travel on the Birthright trip along with senior Hillel staff. The interns will often run social and educational events on campus before and after the trip, along with other engagement opportunities offered by Hillel professionals. The SJE or another senior member of the Hillel staff serve as mentors for the interns.

2) A return trip to Israel.

Research conducted for Masa Israel (Cohen & Kopelowitz, 2010) shows similar dramatic differences between BRI alumni who participate in post programming and those that do not. In this case, the post trip experience is provided by a second trip to Israel. BRI participants who return to Israel for a second trip are far more engaged with Israel and Jewish life than those who do not return; and, those who return on a longer trip are more engaged than those who return on a shorter trip. *Indeed those BRI participants who do not return on a second Israel trip, do not look too different in terms of their Jewish involvements than other young adult American Jews who did not participate on BRI.*

In sum, the Hillel and MASA research points to the importance of what happens after the return from Israel. If there is no follow-up framework the trip becomes a positive memory, and not a platform for significant commitment to engaging with Jewish life and/or increased Jewish practice. In contrast, when an individual is provided the opportunity to act on the heightened feeling of emotional connection to Israel, there is a far greater chance of profound long-term impact.

NOTES FOR EDUCATORS ON
INTEGRATING ISRAEL

This section of the book has explored ways of integrating Israel more deeply and more broadly into Jewish life through a wide array of Jewish educational experiences. We began in Vignette 1 by providing an organizing framework for thinking about Israel education across time and space. As we noted, all too often, it seems that the subject matter and representations of Israel remain episodic and ceremonial. This first vignette is offered as a way to help expand our thinking about when, where, and how Israel can be integrated into the various dimensions of learning. While the focus of the vignette itself is on day schools, the same dimensions we describe can apply to other educational settings and experiences as well. The remaining vignettes in this section consider what integration might look like from different educational perspectives and contexts. What they hold in common is a shared commitment to the idea that the effectiveness and long-term impact of Israel education is strongly linked to the ability to integrate Israel studies and Israel experiences more fully with the overall educational enterprise and the Jewish lives of its participants.

The idea of integration as an educational goal has its roots in the work of John Dewey who advocated connecting students' life experiences with wider social issues. His focus was on the here and now of the educational process as reflected in his oft quoted statement that education "is a process of living and not a preparation for future living" (Dewey, 1897/1992, p. 364). Building on Dewey's work, theories of constructivism in education posit that people learn by building on and enriching existing knowledge and experience. Accordingly, to be effective, Israel education must do a better job of integrating Israel into what American Jews already know and do (Grant, 2007). This was brought to life in Vignette 2 by showing how the Proficiency Approach builds curriculum based on the students' interests and life experiences. Dewey's principle of building on experience can also be seen in Vignette 3's finding that the greatest promise for creating a more Israel-engaged congregation begins with the "committed core" of members who already actively express Jewish commitments and behaviors.

The vignettes also reinforce Malkus' (2011) suggestion that we need to think about the challenges of integration in Jewish educational settings through two different lenses: instructional/curricular and institutional culture. Through the former, are issues relating to instructional strategies and the role of teachers as curriculum developers and implementers. Institutional culture relates to factors that either promote and enhance integration or serve as barriers to its implementation.

While significant research has been done about the curricular and cultural challenges of integrating Jewish studies with general studies (Bekerman & Kopelowitz, 2007; Lehman, 2008, Levisohn, 2008; Lukinsky, 1978; Malkus, 2001, 2011; Solomon, 1978; Zeldin, 1992), very little research has been done about the integration of Israel as subject matter and value within the Jewish (or general studies) domain. Vignette 2 provides a taste of how this might be done through Hebrew language instruction. The JCDS approach to "Hebrew throughout the day" helps to make Hebrew not only a subject to be mastered but a value to internalize that reflects a deep connection to the language and culture of Israel.

A Proficiency Approach to Hebrew language instruction combined with deliberate attention to Hebrew and its place in the symbols, structures, and lived experiences of school is clearly a powerful way to richly and organically foster Jewish identities that internalize a strong sense of engagement with and connection to Israel. However, Hebrew is not the sole avenue for achieving a more integrative approach. Indeed, Vignette 3 that focuses on the synagogue shows the potential for integrating Israel into a variety of different dimensions of synagogue life in a way that is sensitive and responsive to the needs and motivations of congregants at different levels of engagement with Jewish life.

What might an integrated approach entail?

On the most fundamental level, integration means making sure Israel is part of the congregational and Jewish communal landscape through formal and informal means, through regular, ongoing conversations, cultural experiences, study, and worship. Integration means finding ways to connect Israel more integrally and organically to things that Jews already do in synagogues and other communal organizations – *Torah*, *Avodah*, and *Gemilut Hasadim*, study, worship, social action, and just plain having fun and socializing with one's peers. Just as layers of meaning can be added to the celebration of the appointed times for the holidays through study of *Torah*, joyful communal worship, festive meals, and acts of loving kindness, so too can Jewish lives be enriched when Israel is integrated into these aspects of how individuals express themselves as Jews. Experiences of *Torah* study and fulfillment of the *mitzvot*, of prayer and communal worship, and of acts of repair and deeds of loving kindness are all enhanced and enriched by connecting to people and place, to the visions and realities that encompass Israel both as sacred symbol and as a dynamic, modern state.

Israel education must consciously create opportunities for multiple *mifgashim* – encounters with Jewish history, with Jewish time and sacred space, with contemporary Israeli culture and politics, and with a plurality of Jewish voices in Israeli society and around the world. In the same spirit, Vignette 3 shows how collaboration on joint Israel education programming between neighboring synagogues and other Jewish communal organizations can serve to strengthen a community's overall understanding of Israel, especially in terms of Jewish Peoplehood.

In reality, most Jewish organizations are far from implementing an integrated approach to Israel education. In a recent study of Reform congregational educators, just under a third of the respondents reported that that Israel education is strongly integrated into their Jewish studies program (Grant, 2007). As yet, there is no comprehensive study of exactly how these schools or synagogues define and actualize integration. Further research to more fully explore the potential of an integrated approach is essential.

As our study of four St. Louis congregations (Vignette 3) shows, success in integrating Israel into the fabric of congregational life varies depending on program area. What this research clearly demonstrated was that the most involved congregants are also the most likely to respond positively to an Israel engagement initiative. In other words, the more Jewishly engaged they were, the more open and interested they were in engaging with Israel. Consistent with our premise that Israel is a portal into richer Jewish life, we argue that these involved congregants will likely, as a result of more intensive Israel engagement, also intensify their involvement in congregational, and hence, Jewish life in general.

Integration must be thoughtfully planned. We cannot just up the ante in terms of how often Israel is mentioned or rely solely on Israeli *shlichim* (emissaries) to bring a taste of Israel to Jewish camps, congregations and schools. Indeed, as we will see in Vignette 2 in the Connect section and the Camp Harlam case study, overreliance on Israeli emissaries to represent Israel can work against integration, keeping Israel as something imported into the educational community for special events or to add a little spice to the routine. Integration requires close and critical examination of curriculum, liturgy, social action programs, and other activities that bring groups of Jews together to see where and how inclusion of Israel fits with the overall program and learning goals. It requires attending to core questions about curricular goals and processes across grade levels and across formal and informal educational settings, including Israel trips. Curricular goals should be set through careful deliberation on three key questions: (1) What does Israel - mythic and real, sacred and contemporary, Land and People, have to do with Jewish experience in the Diaspora? (2) How can an understanding of the multiple dimensions of Israel as *Am, Torah, Eretz, U'Medinah* enrich one's experiences as a Jew? and (3) What is our stance at a personal level, educators and students alike, towards the character of Israeli society and its implications for our lives?

An example of this type of process was an initiative of MAKOM, The Jewish Agency's Israel Engagement Network, involving a mix of Reform and Conservative congregations and other Jewish communal organizations that took place in four different communities throughout the U.S in 2007-2009. During the initial phase of the process, the congregations engaged in a comprehensive mapping of the place of Israel in their congregations: through formal curriculum, Israel trips, Israel committees, cultural and educational programming, worship, social action initiatives, etc. The process was designed to help congregational leaders identify and understand what are the Israel narrative(s) currently present in the congregation. What predominates? What is the mix? How often and where does Israel appear as a safe haven, as sacred center, as a country in conflict, as a mythic place of heroes and miracles (ancient and modern), as a center of Jewish cultural innovation, as a society filled with social, economic, political, and religious tensions, as a community with a shared destiny with Jews around the world?

This analytical process was designed to help congregational leaders reflect on how broadly or narrowly Israel appears in formal and informal educational experiences in the congregation. It was intended to lead them to assess whether their programming fits with espoused and implicit goals, and identify areas needing greater (or lesser) emphasis. Finally, it was intended to help them make the implicit more explicit and clarify priorities for more fully integrating Israel into all aspects of congregational life.

This method of rigorous self-assessment has been adopted elsewhere. For instance, the Leadership Institute, a UJA-Federation of NY funded program jointly run by the Hebrew Union College and the Jewish Theological Seminary, includes a 12-day Israel seminar as part of its two and a half year curriculum. In preparation for the experience, the 40 participating congregational principals complete an "Israel audit" of their school and congregation, applying the methodologies developed by MAKOM. This both greatly increases their awareness of the multi-dimensional presence of Israel across space and time in their setting, and it helps them enter the Israel seminar with greater discernment about the questions and activities they want to explore while on the trip.

The final vignette of this section focused on what happens after the Israel trip. Here, our primary message is that the trip is essential but insufficient for integrating Israel into Jewish life as lived on an ongoing basis. The trip ignites sparks but without feeding the flames, the embers of excitement will diminish and perhaps even die over time. Thus, there is a critical need for follow-up to help participants reflect and consider how the Israel experience connects and has the potential to enrich one's life on an ongoing basis.

The integration of Israel with Judaism is hardly a new idea. It is embedded throughout the liturgy and Jewish calendar. Sacred texts are permeated with references to the landscape, climate, history, and theology of the Land. It is both an idealized homeland, and a complicated, often contentious and difficult to understand political and social reality. It can serve both as a sacred symbol of moral striving and a unifying force for the Jewish People. While at some idealized past time in the past, these values might have been an inherent part of Jewish identity formation, it is not typically the case for much of North American Jewry today who are inclined towards more personalized and customized forms of Jewish engagement that attenuate a sense of collective engagement (Gans, 1994). Thus, more deliberate steps need to be taken by educational institutions to bring what once might have been an organic and integral part of Jewish life to a more active and vital place in Jewish experience. We hope these vignettes have begun to show just how that might be achieved.

II. COMPLICATE: FROM REFLEXIVE
COMMITMENT TO MATURE LOVE

Ask a Jewish educator what the purpose of teaching Israel ought to be, and you are likely to get an answer something like "to teach them to love Israel." Yet, can we really teach love? Doesn't one have to have first-hand experience of someone or something in order to fall in love? Love is hardly a rational experience, at least at first. Amos Oz states in an oft-quoted poem that you cannot "educate to love." Perhaps, he continues, you can "infect" someone with love, and there is ample evidence that this occurs, at least for the short-term, for many participants on organized Israel trips. But, he concludes by reminding us that "love can be awakened, but not with a strong hand, not with an outstretched arm, and not with burning anger – rather through an approach of mutuality" (Oz, 1981). Myth and miracle may have their place in igniting passion, but an enduring relationship is fostered through mutuality, through constant care, attention, including learning to adapt and compromise.

Unfortunately, the teaching of Israel in North American Jewish education has been much more often about the myth and miracle than it has been about the work of creating a relationship of mutuality based on deep knowing and rich understanding. Indeed, for decades, educational researchers and thinkers have observed that the goals for teaching Israel are "low-level and ambiguous ....reflect[ing] no ideological principles beyond the assumption that Israel is important, nor do they delineate any clear sense of meaning of Israel for Jewish life" (Chazan, 1979, p. 8).

While not always explicitly stated, the impetus for a renewed focus on Israel today appears framed largely around a survivalist impulse that laments a growing rate of intermarriage and assimilation with the attendant consequences of weakened and eroded Jewish identity (Charmé & Zelkowitz, 2011). Education about Israel has been offered up as a solution to strengthen

Jewish belonging and stem the tide of this loss. In this way, Israel has become an instrument or a tool to reinforce *American* Jewish identity and facilitate group cohesiveness. This is most obviously and strenuously played out on Israel trips for teens and young adults but can also be evidenced in how Israel is taught in summer camps, day schools and congregational settings. Following this logic, Israel needs to be presented in a positive light in order to cultivate attachment and excitement about belonging.

While these are desirable outcomes, the means of promoting positive Jewish identity and commitment to group life typically produce an orientation to subject matter and experiences of Israel that primarily focus on the symbolic level so that they can remain consistent with American conceptions of "Zion as it ought to be" (Sarna, 1996). We create larger-than-life representations of Israel through episodic and rather superficial encounters. We avoid problematizing or over-complicating in order to ensure a love of Israel. But by doing so, we are left without addressing the core question of why Israel is or should be significant in American Jewish life.

The implications for Jewish identity are evident in how Israel is taught in classrooms, at Jewish summer camps, and how it is represented on trips. In his research on Birthright Israel, Kelner (2010) notes how these trips succeed in fostering a unitary conception of self, which is at odds with a far more complicated reality where multiple identities comfortably co-exist. "Being Jewish" in everyday life is experienced in a fluid, dynamic and often fragmented fashion; a reality, which Jewish educators try to counter with experiences that build cohesion and lessen the power of "competing identities."   But what of the "return home?"   When participants leave the classroom, camp or Israel trip are they in a position to act on their strengthened sense of Jewish self once back on home turf? Does the Jewish educational experience speak to their everyday life? Does Jewish education endure?

Likewise, what is the price we should be willing to pay for a strong Jewish identity? If Jewish education means over-simplifying and avoiding dissonance, then it does a disservice to the individual as a critical thinker and goes against the experience of life as it is actually lived. If we accept that one of the hallmarks of liberal education in American society is the value placed on developing the capacity to question, to examine issues from multiple perspectives, and to explore a variety of cultures (Nussbaum, 1997), then these same skills and capacities need to be applied to Jewish education in general, and Israel education in particular. Ironically, cultivating such skills and capacities may reveal an uncomplicated Israel experience as incomplete, biased, or in the extreme, fraudulent. Israel education demands that we negotiate the tensions between engagement with and commitment to Israel while at the same time being able to grapple with nuance and complexity in ways that allow for challenge, critique, and individual perspective.

Research shows that many Jewish educators are reluctant to challenge students to engage in the kind of critical thinking that is typical of general studies classes in secondary and higher education (Hyman, 2008; Tanchel, 2006). Studies suggest that there are educators who are themselves reluctant to enter into this kind of terrain for fear that their own conceptions of and commitments to Israel may be challenged (Sinclair, Backenroth, and Bell-Kligler, 2010. Indeed, it appears that the desire to cultivate a sense of deep connection and embeddedness in Jewish tradition may override the educational impulse to question tradition with the goal of bringing Judaism into life in a personally meaningful way. On the one hand, there appears to be a growing recognition that it is not only possible, but desirable for Jewish educators to teach learners how to navigate the tensions of a complex world of multiple identities and open inquiry, as a Jew. Likewise, many educators and policy makers may be ready to accept that "the Jewish community needs to go beyond cheerleading, fundraising and defending the Jewish State from its many critics" (Weiner, 2010) in order to seriously engage American Jews in meaningful conversations about and connections to Israel. On the other hand, even among those individuals and institutions at the forefront of programmatic development and innovation, few are able to articulate a clear vision or purpose for teaching Israel that extends beyond the symbolic plane. And, for the most part, it appears that many Jewish educators still teach old conceptions, old narratives, because they don't know what else to do. Indeed, it seems that a tacit assumption is made that only by first cultivating an uncritical "love of Israel" can we hope to engage Diaspora Jews at all.

It may well be that embracing the complexity of Jewish belonging, and Israel within that weave, flies in the face of educators who strive to instill a "love" of Israel. Many educators fear that revealing too many of Israel's complexities may alienate students and undermine formation of a strong Jewish identity. Indeed, a strong argument can be made for the need to cultivate a sense of connection and commitment before inviting a more critical approach. Yet, a conventional approach to education about Israel that promotes and perhaps even demands an unreflective love, may ultimately leave Israel as a superficial, peripheral, and even an alienating aspect of American Jewish life (Ackerman, 1996; Chazan, 2005; Grant, 2007, 2008; Pomson & Dietcher, 2010).

A compelling illustration of the shortcomings of this unreflective approach was given by Israel educator Steve Israel in an account of his visit to a group of middle school boys at an Orthodox American Jewish day school. The rabbi at the school introduced him, by saying that he "had come to talk to them about the Israel that they loved." When the rabbi left the room, Israel asked the students if it was really true that they all loved Israel. At first, they answered "yes," but when he probed, the students told him "it was a school policy to love Israel." As Israel recounted:

When I made it clear that they could really speak their mind and asked them how they really felt about Israel and whether they really loved it, many 'broke down' and confessed that these were things they had been taught to say and some said they felt guilty that they didn't really love Israel the way they were 'meant to'" (Israel, 2008, p. 34).

The model of Israel education that is at the heart of this book, proposes that love should not be the starting point, but rather the ultimate goal. And, it should not be a naïve and unreflective love, but rather a mature love that can endure even in the face of missteps and imperfection. Cultivating mature love requires deep engagement with the complex and rich dimensions of Israel as a Land, People, and State. More importantly, mature love requires a commitment to the Jewish collective enterprise of building a shared future that recognizes our diversity of stories, experiences, beliefs, and practices, and contributes to a thriving Jewish People and a better world.

Educating towards a mature love does not preclude establishing a strong emotional base for Israel engagement at a young age. Indeed, this is an essential first step. As R.S. Peters (1970) noted in his classic work on moral development, habit precedes reason and understanding. In other words, it is necessary to first induct learners into a particular world of knowledge, emotion and action of which Israel engagement is an integral part of Jewish life. As Meyer (2003) writes: "The goal is to draw the child into the circle, not so much to educate (in the sense of drawing out) as to 'instill' a sense of what it is like to live within the circle. Choice then follows after commitment" (p. 154). However, after induction into the circle, there is an immediate need to move learners from the simplicity of initial knowledge and emotion on which Jewish life is anchored, to the complexity of mature adult life upon which Jewish life depends. From the perspective of Israel education, the accepted norms of "the circle" cannot rely solely on ceremony and myth. These must become part of a broader pantheon that includes knowledge, opinion and action on the very real challenges that are at the heart of Israeli society today and the impact of that reality on the life of Diaspora Jews. If a model of mature love is experienced as the norm from a young age, then caring about Israel is taken to a higher plane, one that incorporates both harmony and conflict as integral to a deep commitment and robust understanding of what it means to be a Jew.

Engagement with Israel must be based on knowledge and interaction, not on platitudes and slogans. While young children may not be ready to fully grasp the deep complexities of history and current events, they can be taught that there are multiple ways to engage with Israel and each of these ways can add value and enrich their lives. They may study sacred texts or engage with cultural expressions as manifest in holiday celebrations, literature, food, and music that foster an appreciation of the cultural, ethnic, religious, and political diversity within the Jewish People, and explore through these prisms the challenges that diversity presents to the modern Israeli state.

Complicating Israel is rooted in the expectation that engaging with Israel is an essential component of Jewish expression. When done well, the Jewish relationship to Israel is nurtured by a democratic tolerance for different positions and an openness to entering into a relationship with people who hold different opinions and act in different ways. The Jewish relationship to Israel is metaphorically analogous to the relationship members of a family have to one another. The ups and downs of family life are emotionally complex and not easily reduced to neat categories and ideological declarations. Healthy family life often includes argument, conflict, and heartache, rooted in love, mutual dependence, and deep human inter-connection. In the same vein, Israel is an integral part of the public life of the Jewish People. As a family must consider others around the dinner table, so the Jewish polity includes Israel. Just as family members may have different practices and beliefs (and even different religions), they can still sit together and engage in civil discourse around core issues of concern, so too does Jewish life include conflict over Israel. The question is can such conflict be managed in a positive, democratic fashion that will keep Jews bound to one another in a relationship of mature love?

Complicating Israel requires leaders, intellectuals, and educators who possess a deep knowledge base about Israel and a commitment to meaningful engagement. Educators in particular, need to have a high tolerance for ambiguity and nuance and be comfortable allowing for a wide array of points of view and degrees of connection to Israel to be expressed and nurtured in their classrooms or other educational settings.

The vignettes in this section explore various dimensions of what it might mean to complicate Israel in instructional settings. They are drawn from research and observations in Jewish day schools across the denominational spectrum, and the Hebrew Union College, the seminary that trains rabbis, cantors, and educators within the Reform Movement of Judaism.

The first vignette lays out key factors that frequently inhibit meaningful engagement with Israel, particularly for Reform Jews studying in Israel as part of their training to become religious leaders. These students encounter challenges for their personal engagement with Israel around core tensions relating to the individual and society, religion and state, and Jews and non-Jews in Israel. The second vignette describes two educational initiatives at the Hebrew Union College that attempt to foster deeper commitments to meaningful engagement by complicating Israel through classroom study and a short-term Israel trip.

The third vignette in this section shifts focus to a community day high school that offers two different Israel courses for its 12th grade that attempt to cultivate a more mature love of Israel by exploring contemporary challenges in Israel society. Finally, we conclude with a vignette guest authored by Alex Pomson, based on research into the attitudes towards Israel among 40 high school juniors attending four different Jewish day schools that cross the denominational spectrum.

VIGNETTE 1: WHEN THE JEWISH PEOPLE AND ISRAEL CONFLICT

The very word "Israel" is a complicated matter with its multiple meanings and associations. In the media, it refers to the modern nation-state. When it appears in the *siddur*, it might be referring to the Jewish collective or to the actual Land of Israel. In the Bible, it might also refer to the collective or to the patriarch Jacob whose name was changed to Israel after he wrestled with the angel. In contemporary parlance, the word לאום (*L'om*), usually translated as nationality, is used in similar fashion to Israel, at times referring to the modern nation-state and at other times referring to the entire Jewish People. Placing an adjective in front of Israel adds to the multiplicity of meanings. *Am Yisrael* can be understood narrowly as the modern nation or more broadly as encompassing all Jews everywhere. Similarly, *Eretz Yisrael* is used both to refer to the land on which the State is situated as well as the sacred land that God promised to Abraham and his descendants.

The ambiguity of the three terms – *Am, Eretz,* and *L'om*, is intentional, signifying the actuality of a rootedness in a particular geographic locale and the aspiration that all Jews are part of the Jewish collective regardless of where they live. A far less ambiguous descriptor is מדינה (*Medina*), the state, which is defined by citizenship. And yet here too, we find some blurred boundaries, literally in terms of the defined and disputed borders of the State of Israel, and figuratively, in terms of considering just who is a part of this civic collective. We see this play out in common parlance. For instance, many of the quasi-governmental agencies that historically have connected Diaspora Jews to Israel: the Jewish Agency, WZO, *Keren Hayesod,* and *Keren Kayemet* (JNF) are referred to as המוסדות הלאומיים (*ha'mosdot hal'umim*) the Nation/People's institutions, not the State's. Likewise, you can see a blurring in the distinction between *Medina* and *L'om* for example, in the name of a parking lot by the Government Center (Supreme Court, Bank of Israel, Prime Minister's Office,

Knesset...): הלאום חניון (*ha-l'om chanyon*), the Nation/People's parking, not "governmental" or "state". And for decades political figures refer regularly to the population of the State of Israel as *Am Yisrael* or even " כל עם ישראל " (the entire *am*/People Israel), despite the fact that more than 20% of Israel's citizenry is not Jewish.

The intentionality of this ambiguity actually conveys a clear message: Israel's raison d'etre is to be the national Homeland for the Jewish People. That is the core purpose for the establishment and ongoing project of nation building within the Jewish state. For many Jews, both in Israel and the Diaspora, Israel serves as an anchor and some would say the center of the Jewish collective experience, the place where Jews can enjoy full equality and express the full measure of their humanity. Others however, reject the notion of Israel as the (or even *a*) center of collective Jewish experience. Indeed, there appears to be a growing number of those who suggest that *Medinat Yisrael* (the state), presents an obstacle to identification and solidarity with *Am Yisrael*, (the Jewish People) and who may even reject the idea that collective Jewish experience is a value worth upholding and acting upon at all.

Attention to these multiple meanings is far more than wordplay when considering the impact on the next generation of North American Jews and Jewish leadership. The same might be said for Israeli Jews as well, although the focus here draws from experiences with young American Jewish adults. Over the last several years, one of our co-authors (Grant) has engaged in serious, substantive, and ongoing conversations about Jewish Peoplehood with rabbinical and education students at the Hebrew Union College. These conversations have been structured around formal and informal encounters with people and ideas with the intent of fostering a greater consciousness about and commitment to *Klal Yisrael*, a less ambiguous term than those already noted, that connotes Jewish Peoplehood without a specific connection to Nationhood. For many of these young adults, *Klal Yisrael* is a foreign and even alienating concept, so it logically follows that the ideas of *Am*, *L'om*, and *Medina* are even more distant from their consciousness and experience.

The students' comments and concerns focus around three core tensions that seem to contribute to this detachment. The first relates to the primacy of the individual over the collective, the second concerns the relationship and tensions between varying streams of Jews, and the third is the relationship and tensions between the Jewish State and the Palestinians.

On the surface, the first of these factors – the primacy of the individual over the collective - may appear to be unrelated to the tension between *Am Yisrael* and *Medinat Yisrael*, but in fact, it does shape foundational perceptions and assumptions about the Jewish collective and Israel as a Jewish State. Most North American Jews today see Judaism as a personal matter, where individual autonomy is privileged over a commitment to a communal set of norms, values, and behaviors. This sentiment is often given expression by the phrase "my Judaism," meaning that Judaism is whatever *I* make it. North American Jews, including these highly engaged and deeply committed future rabbis and educators, feel fully comfortable choosing whether, when, where, and how to connect to Jews and Jewish beliefs and practice. They also prefer communities with porous and fluid boundaries between Jews and non-Jews. For them, this is normative, which is hardly the case in Israeli society today.

Such conflicts between personal autonomy and the power of what is perceived and often acts as a hegemonic religious authority in Israeli society is a key factor that gives rise to what Mordecai Nisan (2009) describes as a "double dissonance." By this, he means the contradiction between one's "love of the group and [one's] discovery of some negative aspects of it; and the contradiction or gap between some views or values in the tradition of the collective (such as attitude toward women) and core components of [one's] personal identity" (p. 35).

This double dissonance arises for many liberal Jews when they come to Israel for an extended period of study. Many arrive with an idealized expectation (often first fostered on a short-term trip) that since "everyone is Jewish" they will feel fully comfortable and welcomed in the Jewish State. In other words, they come with a predisposition to feel welcomed and included because they are Jewish. Instead, they are confronted with different cultural norms from what they expected, ranging from rude behavior, to complex bureaucratic systems, to outright derision, especially towards young women who wear *kippot* in public or even those who simply reveal that they are studying to become rabbis. Thus, while they may come to Israel with a romanticized "love of the group," their actual encounters are often shaped by these negative first impressions.

The second aspect of the dissonance – concerning the relationship between the State of Israel and the varying streams of Jews - is an even more profound value conflict. Most American Jews understand a clear separation between church and state as a means of protecting freedom of religion. Yet, in Israel, the Jewish State, they feel their own religious expression is restricted because of the political power held by Orthodox religious authorities who impose their understandings of appropriate religious behavior on the entire population. This relates to relatively minor annoyances such as the lack of public transportation and commerce on Shabbat and holidays, to what is perceived as far more insidious control over public funding for non-Orthodox synagogues and educational programs, gender-segregated bus lines and other restrictions on women's public behavior, and the ultimate arbiter of defining just who is a Jew.

The dissonant experience arises when these young adult Jews come to Israel for their first year of graduate studies at HUC. Many encounter disdain for Reform Judaism and Reform Jews both from *Am Yisrael*, the Jewish Nation/People and *Medinat Yisrael*, the Jewish State. They experience this in informal conversations and in the public square. At the extreme, they are sworn at and spat upon. This occurs as reported in chance encounters, and with some regularity at the *Kotel* during "Women at the Wall" *Rosh Chodesh* services. In a more benign fashion, they are simply dismissed as inauthentic, ignorant, and non-*halachic*. Their response is one of alienation and profound hurt that often gets expressed in the retort: "Why should I want to feel connected to *Klal Yisrael* when there are many in that collective who reject that I'm studying to be a rabbi and maybe won't even accept that I'm a Jew?"

A third tension that informs their experience of Israel concerns the relationships and attitudes of *Am Yisrael*, the Jewish Nation/People, towards the Palestinians, both those who are citizens of *Medinat Yisrael*, the Jewish State, and those who are stateless in the West Bank and Gaza. For many of these students, social justice activism is a core aspect of their Jewish identity. Thus, many express profound disappointment and confusion when they confront a complex and difficult reality where a sizable minority of Israel's own citizens (not to mention Palestinians who are under Israeli governmental control) are denied equal access to the full measure of rights and opportunities afforded to Jewish citizens of the state. In essence, the question they ask is: "How can Israel live up to its ideal as a 'light unto the nations' when it systematically and consistently discriminates against 20% of its own population?" Indeed, they even perceive, perhaps correctly, that most Jewish Israelis are content to continue such discriminatory policies in the fear that providing fair and equal access to Palestinian citizens of Israel will undermine the Jewish nature of the state.

These tensions are real and are seen by many as irreconcilable. However, they are discussed and deliberated upon in a variety of settings, including the weekly Israel seminar, monthly reflection groups that are designed to help students grapple with key questions about Israel and Jewish Peoplehood, and of course, in informal conversations among students. While this brief presentation does not allow for detailed elaboration of these educational strategies, what is clear is that thoughtful and deliberative educational experiences can re-frame polarizing tensions as formative ones that invite learners to engage in serious and productive grappling with their attitudes and understandings of the interrelationships and conflicts between *Am, Eretz,* and *Medinat Yisrael.* It requires open and honest exploration of ambiguities and complexities through encounters, experiences, dialogue, and reflection both with like-minded and culturally compatible peers as well as with individuals and groups who are markedly different in world view, life style, and culture. Working through such tensions in a formative way challenges one to opt in to being part of the politics of the Jewish public sphere in order to influence it. That is the difference between a stance of "my Judaism" and a commitment to live as a member of the Jewish collective that, after all, is the ultimate goal in creating a thriving and more connected Jewish world.

VIGNETTE 2: COMPLICATING ISRAEL IN THE CLASSROOM AND ON THE ROAD

An abundance of survey research explores the beliefs, attitudes, and relationships of American Jews to Israel. In recent years, two schools of scholarship have engaged in a vigorous debate about whether younger American Jews are growing increasingly distant from Israel or whether in fact the impact of Birthright Israel has had the opposite effect. One camp credits the rise of intermarriage, assimilation, and a general disconnect of American Jewry from Jewish life as the factors that contribute to this distancing (Cohen & Kelman, 2006, 2010). The other camp, claims that distancing from Israel is not occurring (Saxe et al., 2008). While such survey data are extremely important in trying to understand broad patterns and trends, when considering how to complicate Israel, it is also quite useful to zoom in more closely through in-depth interviews and other qualitative methods that reveal more nuance and detail about attitudes and behaviors. This vignette offers two examples of this type of close-in examination of options, reflections, questions, and beliefs of young North American Jews. The first example reports on interviews about attitudes and beliefs towards Zionism with a group of seven American Jews in their twenties living in Israel, between 2005 and 2010. The second example focuses on the impact of two different experiences at the Hebrew Union College, an Israel travel seminar for MA students in Jewish education, and a semester-long course given on the college's New York campus called "Why Israel Matters."

Constructing a Usable Zionism through a Break with the Past

In 2007, Grant conducted a series of in-depth interviews with seven different American Jews who were living in Israel, for one year or longer. All were in their mid-to-late twenties. One was an Israeli citizen who moved to the U.S. when he was seven and returned to Israel to attend graduate school. Two were in Israel for a year or more of study, two had made *aliyah*, and two others were living and working in Israel but had consciously chosen not to make *aliyah*. Some intended to make their lives in Israel, others were there for a fixed time and purpose, and still others were uncertain. Four of the seven lived in Tel Aviv or Jaffa, two in Jerusalem, and one was studying in a Yeshiva in Efrat. One had secular Israeli parents, one grew up centrist Orthodox, and five grew up in the Conservative movement. While hardly a scientific sample they are representative of those young American Jews who are among the most committed to Israel and the Jewish People. Thus, it is worth paying attention to what they say about their choices and how they understand themselves in relationship to the Jewish State.

One of the questions put to this group was to define their personal understanding of Zionism. Most of the answers began in traditional ways: "being proud of our Jewish State," "the right for all Jews to live in Israel," "the belief that there is a connection of Jews to Israel, whatever that connection might be". However, two of the respondents appeared to reject Zionist ideology outright. In most of the other cases, the respondents went on to qualify or juxtapose a classical belief of Zionism with a more critical reflection on contemporary reality. Below are three examples of how these young adults are grappling with this tension.

Zionism is a belief that Israel is a place, a home for all Jews - should they ever choose to live there. Ideally, a 'Homeland' that is at peace within its own borders and with its neighbors. My Zionism is not 'exclusive.' I believe that it is possible to care about your own family and 'People' and still have room to care about other people and other nations as well.

To me, 'Zionism' is an antiquated term that is anachronistic and is in desperate need of being redefined. To me it is simply the support of the existence of the State of Israel, and there are many countless ways to support the State, from environmental protection to supporting education of Arab Israeli girls.

Zionism means an ideology that advocates the right of all Jews to settle in Israel. It is an ideology that I was brought up, learned from my family, synagogue and Camp Ramah, and one that I have struggled with immensely in recent years. I find it problematic to the point where it is now difficult for me to identify with the ideology because I believe it has been used to discriminate against non-Jews and turn Israel into a problematic society.

From these quotes, we see that these young adults have not exactly rejected the past but instead are trying to reconcile their desire for and commitment to a Jewish Homeland in Israel, with their vision of a more just and equitable society for all its citizens. For them, old conceptions of Israel as a safe haven, a model state, and a "light unto the nations" are no longer valid descriptors of the Jewish State. They may still see them as ideals to strive for, but they recognize that there is a huge gap between myth and reality. From their remarks, it appears that they are attempting to reconcile these obsolete conceptions with the complexities and imperfections of contemporary Israel. In effect, they are striving to construct a "usable past" that is simultaneously critical and yet committed to the project of *tikkun*, repair. Each may have a different conception of what that *tikkun* would entail, ranging from the "belief that Jews have a right (on various levels) to live in the Land of Israel (whatever that means...)" or the opinion that "Jews can belong here along with other people." One took a much more critical stance, rejecting the Zionist ideology that embraces the idea of The Greater Land of Israel, most commonly associated with the Settler movement:

The Zionism I struggle with is the belief that this is a Jewish Homeland and therefore Jews are valued first and foremost as well as the land from the

Euphrates to the Nile is Jewish land and therefore needs to remain or, in the future be, in Jewish hands.

Yet, even the most critical post-Zionist in the group, acknowledges a deep connection to Israel as these comments suggest:

I continue to struggle with an intense love/hate relationship, but it is something that challenges me, keeps me interested and makes me want to stay engaged with the issues…… I remain drawn to Israel because I feel it continues to play a central role in my Jewish identity. I feel inextricably tied to the country as it defines itself, and also, therefore, feel responsible for its actions in the name of the Jewish People (be it with pride or shame).

The thoughts and feelings shared by these young adults can be characterized as representative of a critical, mature, and self-reflective relationship with Israel. As educators, our ultimate goal may still be "love of Israel;" however, we should strive to cultivate a mature love rather than a naïve one. We should neither whitewash nor ignore the complexities of contemporary Israel. We can and even should still teach the old "myths" as ideals, but we must do so in a way that makes them usable in tension with current realities.

This approach can best be characterized as a form of critical engagement with Israel. This phrase embodies the richness and weight of an Israel that is multi-layered with historical, religious, political, cultural, social, and existential significance, making it wholly problematic and tremendously complicated. Rather than over-simplify or avoid these tensions, this approach confronts them. Just as we accept that troublesome texts in our sacred tradition must be wrestled with rather than excised, so too should we grapple with those aspects of Israel that leave us uneasy and perplexed. Granted, educational processes that negotiate these tensions are more complicated and nuanced, but ultimately they can provide a rich foundation of content, knowledge, and experiences. Indeed, one could even make the argument that cultivating the ability to negotiate such tensions is not only an educationally sound strategy, but is also an essential component of what it means to be a Jew in the modern world.

Critical Engagement in a Reform Seminary

Almost all students at the Hebrew Union College spend their first year of studies in Jerusalem, where in addition to Hebrew language, 20% of the curriculum is devoted to tours, meetings, seminars, lectures and encounters with different aspects of Israeli society, geography and history. A handful of these students spend significant time studying or volunteering in Israel prior to attending HUC. Others have been to Israel on visits, through their synagogue, youth group, and/or camp. Each year, there are also a small number of students who have never been to Israel before, making their year in Israel at HUC their first experience.

Clearly, the most intensive period of time in which HUC students directly experience and engage with Israel is during their year of studies there. When they return to the U.S. campuses Israel tends to fade into the background as other academic studies and internships take precedence. But there are opportunities for students to continue to remain critically engaged through a variety of formal and informal means. Among those, are two activities that one of us is responsible for: a semester-long course entitled "Why Israel Matters" and a bi-annual twelve-day seminar in Israel. The course is designed to provide a forum for students to grapple intellectually, emotionally, and spiritually with their knowledge of and relationship to Israel and what this means to them as American Jews. Each class session is designed as a multi-layered encounter between the idealized visions and the complex, dynamic, and always challenging realities that shape our understandings and connections to Israel. We use primary sources, scholarly articles, literature, film, visual images, and music to consider four closely related conceptions of *Am, Torah, Eretz* and *Medinah* as a sacred symbol and a living polity. Ample class time is devoted to address questions of personal meaning and to help students articulate a strategic vision for why and how to teach Israel from the pulpit, at camps, in the classroom and other settings where Jews gather to learn.

Below are several written reflections by different students taken from writing assignments that ask them to engage intellectually and personally with the ideas presented and discussed in the class. Studied carefully, they show the engagement with ideas and the type of learning that takes place in this class.

This class pushed me to define what Zionism means to me. At this point, I would say that Zionism is an engagement with Israel- its politics, language, arts and culture- that ultimately ends in supporting the idea of a Jewish State that upholds human rights for all its citizens, while allowing critique. I think this definition shows many of the issues that I have grappled with thus far in my life: What does it mean to be engaged with Israel, what are my own entry points into loving Israel? What is our Jewish responsibility to critique Israel? What does a 'Jewish democracy' mean? And how do I describe the Israeli-Palestinian conflict in a way that affirms human rights? I'm still thinking about answers to these questions, but these are part of my personal Zionist struggle.

When we got to the discussion about Reform Zionism, there was great pain in the room. Many of us expressed a longing for clarity and certainty, both things that were decidedly absent from the feelings that we shared about Israel and its place in our Jewish identities. Reform Zionism, and my Zionism, is a collection of Zionisms, sometimes shifting and contradictory, that result in a shaky whole that is reflective of our contemporary context.

Reflecting on the course, I realized that there are many things that in my entire year of living in Israel, I failed to accomplish. The class pushed me to come up with improved answers to what Zionism means to me. Zionism is something that has always had a very special place for me, a place right in the back of my mind. But how can I teach effectively about it when I myself know so little about it? I spent a lot of time this year thinking about Israel in a complex way, trying to disconnect my own personal experience of Israel from the larger study of Israel. I think this is my struggle with dualism, the difference between my Israel and actual Israel. It's important to make the distinction because we all want to project our own hopes and dreams onto the State of Israel as a testing ground for the rest of world Jewry and perhaps the world as a whole. Instead, I think that we tend to project unreasonable standards onto this small relatively new country. While it certainly does not excuse the negative actions that Israel has taken over the years, it does remind me that every country makes bad decisions, similarly to human beings.

From my own experiences leading five different Birthright trips and from the research and the narratives presented by Kelner, I question if Taglit is creating a new type of Zionism, a Zionism that promotes a blind love of Israel, where Jews in the Diaspora feel Israel is an insurance plan, just in case anti-Semitism becomes rampant and Jews need a place to escape. Has Birthright-Israel created a program where flying blue and white flags at a mega event or a climb up Masada and yelling 'Am Yisrael Chai' at the top of one's lungs are expressions of one's Zionism? Has Taglit created a program where participants are isolated if one questions the actions of the Israeli government? If the answers are yes, then the Zionism that I described above, could fit with the charges made by Peter Beinart in his article, 'The Failure of the Jewish Establishment', that Jewish organizations are promoting an uncritical brand of Zionism that is detrimental to the Jewish world.

These thoughtful reflections show how the students strive to place their own experiences in Israel (good and bad) in a broader context. They also show how the students develop a deeper sense of nuance and sophistication and become, if not comfortable, at least accepting of the ambiguity and challenges of integrating Israel into their lives as Reform Jews. Indeed, one of the most poignant aspects of the class is when students have the opportunity to talk about where Israel fits into their own Jewish identity. Typically, within each class, a small minority of students unambiguously state that Israel is central to who they are. A similar number on the opposite end note that while they know that Israel *should* be an essential part of who they are, they just don't feel it. The majority of students in between these two poles express in one way or another the feeling that they would like Israel to be more integrated but they just don't see how it fits into their daily lives as Reform American Jews. One of the reasons why they choose to take this course is their hope that it will provide them with the understandings to make Israel a more integral aspect of their lives.

****

The bi-annual Israel seminar for students is organized around a theme that is developed through a series of encounters with land, texts, and people to fit with the theme. Most of the students who participate on this trip have been to Israel before, and some have even been staff on teen or Birthright trips. There are also a handful of students who have never been on an organized trip. Regardless of their personal Israel experiences, none of the students have been on a trip oriented particularly to educators in the making. The learning is largely experiential and integrated, meaning it is designed to connect study about and experience of Israel with Jewish beliefs and values, and Jewish practice. The goal is to develop a deep and multi-layered appreciation for thinking about and teaching Israel as an integrated and integral component of Jewish life wherever it is lived. The program strives to model creative educational experiences that ask participants to grapple with "formative tensions" between myth and reality, Israel and Diaspora, sacred and profane, religion and People, time and space. In keeping with the orientation of this seminar as professional development, participants are asked to take responsibility for developing certain aspects of the program. During seminars students give *divrei Torah*, lead services, and create reflection sessions at relevant moments. In one seminar, for example, two students volunteered to create a closing ceremony after a visit to *Yad VaShem* to serve as a way to reflect on the experiences in the museum and memorial sites. This took place about two-thirds of the way through the trip. The day before the visit, however, one of the student facilitators acknowledged that even though she volunteered eagerly for this assignment before the trip, now she found she was totally ill-equipped to guide the group through a meaningful reflection.

This was a student who had extensive experience in informal education through Jewish camping and leading NFTY and

Birthright Israel trips. Yet, as she reported, the experiences of this Israel seminar had made her aware of how little she really knew or understood about Israel. She felt that all of her prior Israel experiences painted a picture of an idealized and mythic Israel, and only through our seminar did she realize how complex and multi-layered the reality was. In her written reflections at the end of the trip, she noted:

While I have great passion for this country, I know that I'm lacking all the resources and a philosophy to help carry it for the Reform movement. I hope this experience will help me begin to lay out ways/create lesson approaches so my participants will find ways for substantive connections to Israel.

The approach to both the academic course and the experiential seminar in Israel is grounded in Michael Marmur's (2007) articulation of a "liberal theology of Israel." In this essay, he proposes a compelling way for liberal Jews to navigate the dissonance and many complexities that are part of the ongoing reality of the Jewish State. He addresses those Jews who are equally committed to "the cultural and religious imperatives of Jewish particularism….and the guiding principles of modernity" (p. 85), two values that are often in tension. Using the metaphor of a fifth cup at the Passover Seder, Marmur proposes the need to develop a sense of "confident inadequacy" embracing or at least living with the tensions, ambiguities, and responsibilities inherent in Jewish sovereignty. He writes: "If Zionism is to mean anything in our day….. [w]e need the confidence to appreciate all that has been achieved so far, and the confidence to acknowledge that which is still at fault" (p. 93). Cultivating this confident and critical disposition requires the ability to hold multiple, and at times, competing truths about what it means to be seriously engaged with Israel. As one student wrote in her paper on Reform Zionism in the "Why Israel Matters" course:

I don't think it is defeatist to suggest that Reform Zionism in our time is bound to be riddled with tensions and contradictions. Israel is a county riddled with tensions and contradictions. But I would not call this an Israeli problem, or even a Jewish problem. Rather, it is the reality of the search to

Lisa Grant and Ezra Kopelowitz

construct meaning in a time when our grand narratives have been exposed as inadequate. We can only hope that today, we are more partially right than we were yesterday.

This is confident inadequacy at its best, which perhaps is the ultimate goal for the development of future religious leaders in a post-modern era.

VIGNETTE 3: COMPLICATING ISRAEL AT A COMMUNITY JEWISH DAY SCHOOL

Complicating Israel is at the heart of how the Kehilah High School[5] approaches Israel education in the 12th grade. This community Jewish high school located in the Northeast region of the United States, has a mission that describes a school that values open, engaged inquiry with a commitment to nurturing students' curiosity, cultivating their imagination, encouraging creative expression, valuing their initiative, and engendering critical thinking skills. While the word pluralism is not employed, this language clearly expresses pluralism both as a core philosophy of the school and as a methodological approach to teaching and learning. A plurality of perspectives and critical analysis are likewise articulated as goals in the Social Studies department where the academic Israel courses are offered.

This vignette is based on a research study at Kehilah High School that took place in the 2008-09 academic year. The key question driving the research was, *How does a pluralistic Jewish curriculum navigate between fostering open inquiry and supporting a commitment to Israel and the Jewish people?* Data for the study were gathered through a series of classroom observations, formal interviews, and conversations with teachers at Kehilah about their approach to Israel education and how it fits with their overall educational philosophy. Observations and interviews were augmented by review of student work and a brief survey about Kehilah students' experiences of and in Israel and their attitudes about the place of Israel in their lives. The survey was administered to all students enrolled in a semester-long Senior Seminar in the spring of 2009. Forty-seven students representing 70% of the senior class responded.

The analysis of data provides a context for exploring how thinking and speaking about Israel plays out in a Jewish

---

5 This vignette is based on an article by Grant, Lisa D., 2011. Pluralistic Approaches to Israel Education, *Journal of Jewish Education*, 77:1, 4-21.

educational setting that espouses a commitment to critical thinking and pluralistic education. Beth Davis[6], the head of the Social Studies department at Kehilah, clearly articulated this commitment when she said, "We are always trying to foster multiple perspectives. We want our students to look at situations from varying points of view, to look for corroboration and evidence to back up their positions. At the same time, we want to engage them, make them more knowledgeable, and connect the learning to their own experience."

These values were brought to bear on the development of two academic courses on Israel that focus on different issues, but each takes a critical approach. Students in the 12th grade of Kehilah choose one or the other of these semester-long courses. One explores contemporary issues of society and culture, religion, and politics in Israel. The second course focuses more exclusively on the Israeli-Palestinian conflict, using a curriculum developed by the Peace Research Institute of the Middle East (PRIME). Originally intended for use in 10th and 11th grade classrooms in Israel and Palestine, it is also available in English[7]. The curriculum presents side-by-side the Israeli and Palestinian narratives of the history of the region from the early 20th century through the First Intifada. The intent is for each student to learn "the narrative of the other, in addition to the familiar own narrative, as a first step toward acknowledging and respecting the other" (Bar-On & Adwan, 2006, p. 312).

Building on this perspective, Aryeh Freed, who teaches the course, crafted a core concept that he regularly reiterated for his students: "Only if Israel and Palestine can really hear each other's narrative is there any chance of peace." In addition to the academic course, seniors participate in a required non-academic Israel Seminar that meets weekly throughout the year. The seminar is designed as a setting where students debate a series of

---

6 Pseudonyms are used for the name of the school and all teachers cited in this vignette

7 Though designed for an Israeli audience, the PRIME curriculum is prohibited for use in Jewish Israeli schools.

core questions such as: "Why do you think you need a Jewish State? What kind of religious state should the Jewish State be? How do you define Jewish in your Jewish State? How do you treat non-Jews in the State? As an American, what role should Israel play in your life?" By grappling with these questions, Rabbi Marc Levy, the seminar leader hopes the students will be able to explore and articulate their own relationship with Israel and understand that there is not a single right way to think about and relate to Israel. As Levy describes it, the goal "isn't about imparting knowledge, but about investigating their own relationship with Israel."

A survey administered to the senior class in May 2009 provides a big-picture overview of students' attitudes, beliefs, and knowledge about Israel and how their classroom learning experiences may have shaped them. The vast majority of students in both classes have at least some degree of familiarity with Israel. Indeed, their level and frequency of Israel connections far exceeds the norm for other American Jewish teens.

Based on the survey responses in 2009, only two of the 47 respondents had never been to Israel. Fully 85% said they have definite plans to visit Israel in the next five years. There seem to be some significant differences between the students in the two different classes, both in terms of their background and connections to Israel prior to the class and how their attitudes were shaped as a result of their learning. Beth Davis observed that for the most part, the students who opted to take the Dual Narratives class tended to be more Israel knowledgeable and experienced than those in the Society in Culture class. Indeed, the survey responses seemed to confirm this observation as respondents enrolled in the Dual Narratives class reported feeling more knowledgeable, having a deeper spiritual connection, and a stronger emotional attachment to Israel than their classmates in the Society and Culture class. A significantly higher percentage of students in Mr. Freed's Dual Narratives class reported that Jews can be both critical and supportive of Israel than their counterparts in Ms. Davis' Society and Culture class. An even greater difference is seen in how the two groups consider the complexity of Israel with 81.9% of Dual Narratives compared to 55.6% of Society and Culture students rating this as a high priority in terms of their beliefs.

The two groups were much more aligned in other dimensions such as Israel being critical to the survival of the Jewish People and Israel as the Homeland of the Jewish People. The final set of questions on the survey asked the students to reflect directly on how their course impacted on their attitudes and beliefs about Israel. The views of the two groups were aligned in a few dimensions. For example, well over 70% of students in both groups said they agreed or strongly agreed that they appreciated learning multiple perspectives about the social, religious, and/or political situation in Israel.

Based on these survey findings, it appears that the students of the Kehillah high school came to their study of Israel with a strong spiritual, emotional, and personal connection to Israel. It also appears that those students with the stronger connections were more interested in grappling with the Israeli-Palestinian conflict, which most likely was a topic they had never studied in a formal way prior to this class. For both groups of students, it seems that intellectual engagement with the complexities and challenges of Israeli society and the Palestinian conflict was lacking prior to their participation in these classes. Although to varying degrees, both groups of students seemed to deeply appreciate the opportunity to engage with these complexities. It challenged them and for some, put them on edge as the results show on the table below.

For a good number – almost half in the Dual Narratives class and more than a third in the Society and Culture class – grappling with these challenging realities made them even more supportive of Israel.

Confronting these issues for the students in the Society and Culture class who were less strongly engaged with Israel prior to coming into the class, left more than half of them ambivalent about their support for Israel. A relatively small 10% of these students in Society and Culture felt that critical engagement made them less supportive, though slightly more than a quarter of those in Dual Narratives indicated as much.

Breakdown of responses to the question: Learning multiple perspectives about the social, religious, and political/or situation in Israel made me more supportive of Israel

% Responding	Dual Narratives	Society & Culture
Agree/Strongly Agree	48%	37%
Unsure	26%	53%
Disagree/Strongly Disagree	26%	11%

For many Jewish educators, fostering a strong commitment to Israel, indeed a love of Israel, is the *sina qua non* of Israel education. The evidence at Kehillah suggests that pluralistic dispositions that invite critical inquiry are not antithetical to cultivating strong commitments to Israel. Also true is that a sizable percent of the students weren't sure how their study of Israel this year shaped their attitudes and conceptions. That statistic may leave some uneasy, but from a developmental perspective, that irritant of uncertainty is a possible prerequisite to deeper learning, that can lead to critical self-reflection and ultimately to constructed knowing, where learners are capable of integrating knowledge and making meaning for themselves. One of the ongoing debates among colleagues and students interested in creating more purposeful Israel education is whether we can teach critical engagement from the outset, or whether we have to foster a naïve and uncritical love of Israel first and only later deconstruct and rebuild it on a more complex and variegated foundation. It is clear that the many of the students at Kehillah have a strong attachment to Israel (76% in Mr. Freed's class and 53% in Ms. Davis' class) but we have no evidence of what their formal or informal Israel education was before they enrolled in one of these two classes and how that attachment was formed. The survey data certainly showed that the courses offered them the opportunity to study about Israel in greater depth and

Lisa Grant and Ezra Kopelowitz

complexity than ever before and that in the main, they appreciated this exposure.

Whether learners need a solid connection to Israel before engaging in a more critical approach remains a question worthy of further study. A related question is a developmental one that is influenced by age as well as intellectual and emotional capacities and dispositions for wrestling with ambiguity, being open to hearing the voice of the "other," and understanding the implications of one's commitments. In other words, what conditions, if any, are necessary before a learner can fruitfully and meaningfully confront and grapple with multiple perspectives and at times, multiple truths? Ultimately, a pluralistic approach to Israel education is far more about cultivating knowledge than it is about cultivating a desire for ongoing engagement. As Amos Oz reminds us, you cannot "educate to love," you can only awaken someone to love through deep knowledge based on mutuality, relationship, and care. Decades of evidence suggest we have hardly succeeded in achieving these goals when it comes to engagement with and learning about Israel in American Jewish classrooms.

In the introduction to this book we provide a historical overview of the changing relationship of American Jews to Jewish life and Israel. With the changes taking place, new educational methods are needed to capture the hearts and minds of American Jews, beyond what has long been the typical approach of many prepared curriculum to focus on the myth and miracle. Can a pluralistic approach cultivate more complicated, richer, and enduring commitments to Israel and the Jewish People than what we see in many Jewish educational settings? There is clearly a need for further research to explore what, where, and how such initiatives may be changing the nature of Israel education in American Jewish educational settings and its impact on learners. This preliminary inquiry into these questions invites further investigation and debate.

VIGNETTE 4: BEYOND THE B-WORD. LISTENING TO HIGH SCHOOL STUDENTS TALK ABOUT ISRAEL. AUTHOR: ALEX POMSON[8]

When interviewing a sample of 40 high school juniors about their experiences of Israel education in their Jewish day schools, one word surfaced repeatedly. It was what our research team came to call the B-word; bias.

In exploring Israel education's complexity, it is worth unpacking why the students in some schools were more inclined to use this term than were those in others.

The project

With funding provided by the AVI CHAI Foundation, a small research team set out in the academic year 2009-2010 to capture the thoughts and feelings about Israel of a sample of high school juniors. Video-interviews were conducted in four Jewish day schools identified as representing distinct types of modern Orthodox and liberal community high schools in North America. The four schools, two of which were K-12 schools and two stand-alone high schools, included a community day school on the west coast ["Community"]; a modern Orthodox day school in the mid-west ["Kook"]; a community day school on the east coast ["Kehilati"]; and a modern Orthodox day school on the east coast ["Soloveitchik"].[9]

The 40 interviewees were selected through careful consultation with educators so as to represent the mix of students in their schools. Students were identified who could be articulate when interviewed and who would not simply be "poster-children" for

---

8 Dr. Alex Pomson is a senior researcher at the Melton Centre for Jewish Education at the Hebrew University. He was founding head of Jewish studies at the King Solomon High School in London, and Koschitzky Family Professor in Jewish teacher education at York University, Toronto. He is co-author of Back to School: Jewish Day School as a Source of Meaning in the Lives of Adult Jews, and co-editor of the International Handbook of Jewish Education.
9 School names and student names are all pseudonyms.

their institution. We were interested in hearing the widest range of opinion in each case.

Differences in what students say about their schools
Substantiating the data's validity, there were sharp but consistent differences between what interviewees from each one of the four schools said their schools taught them about Israel. At Community, the west coast high school, half of the students interviewed made mention of Israel's complexity, stating explicitly that this is a central aspect of what their school teaches about Israel, an orientation that is congruent both with the school's responsiveness to its students' demographic and ideological diversity and with Israel's contested place in local civic culture. In contrast, the concept of Israel's complexity was almost completely absent from what students at Kehilati, the east coast community day school, said they were taught. Instead, at this school – one widely recognized for its rich Israel programming and strong Israel advocacy culture - more than half of the sample talked about being taught to appreciate what they referred to as Israel's "importance."

At the modern Orthodox schools, complexity didn't figure in what any of these students said their schools addressed. Although some did talk about being taught about Israel's importance, many more revealed a wrestling with or a celebration of (immigration to Israel) as a central Jewish value. At Kook, the mid-west modern Orthodox school, all of the students spoke about *aliyah* as something they talk and think about. At Soloveitchik, the east coast modern Orthodox school, the interviewees indicated that *aliyah* is an important matter in their context too, but in their case they were aware of their school's lack of clarity about something they understood to be important.

The students' reports confirm what we know from other research: that the purposes and practices of Israel education differ sharply between liberal and modern Orthodox day schools, and that, in turn, the particular Jewish cultures of schools are strongly colored by their communal contexts. In liberal and community day schools there is a tension between presenting Israel as a value of singular importance for Jews or as an issue of complexity with which Jews ought to engage. In modern Orthodox schools the tension revolves around the centrality of *aliyah* for religiously observant Jews in the Diaspora.

Similarities in how students talk

While interviewees might indicate that their schools pursue sharply different approaches in how they both present Israel and talk about it, nevertheless, as adolescents, they process their own ideas about Israel in similar kinds of ways. When asked about where they get their ideas about Israel, students in all four schools communicated a preference for relying on their own resources or at least for relying on sources to which they had turned voluntarily. A great many, regardless of location, indicated a preference for learning about Israel from peers in the US and in Israel, from their own inquiries especially on the internet, or through interaction with adults outside school, primarily within their own extended families.

These general tendencies - as well as subtle but ultimately significant differences between students at the community and modern Orthodox schools - are well demonstrated by comparing the comments of Robert and Bradley, two especially articulate students who come from homes where there is frequent and lively talk about Israel. Robert, from the Soloveitchik School clarified how his opinions about Israel have taken shape:

*I like to believe that I form my own opinions about Israel....I read the New York Times every day. I read the Jerusalem Post. And I discuss Israel a lot with my parents...I try to find the reality in whatever the situation is because sometimes that's not so easy to find because I don't believe there is such a thing as being entirely objective. I think that's impossible because we're human beings. So I try to find the truth for myself. I don't really trust anyone else. I trust them to tell me **what**. I don't trust them to tell me **why** or **how**.*

When Robert was pushed by the interviewer about where school fits in to this picture, he continued: "I don't regard my teachers any more as sources of information than I do anyone else because they also have their personal biases". For Robert, then, his teachers are as suspect as any other human being, but not necessarily more so.

Bradley, a student at Community (on the west coast), probes a similar set of issues. He too draws critically on a variety of sources of information; his family also plays an important role in the development of his thinking, but his critique of his teachers, although at first framed much as Robert's was, is sharper because of what he perceives as his teachers' agenda. He explained that, as he has grown older:

I've been more challenging of my school or my teachers' opinions, because it is just one person's opinion…Trusting an expert who might be someone who's writing an article or trusting my family who I can have dialogue with and try to figure out why they have these opinions, is a much better place to get information or to think about Israel than from teachers or school or other people that are clearly biased and are just trying to convince you of something.

The similarities in how these two young men speak underline a core value shared by a great many of those we interviewed. It is a view succinctly expressed by Noah, another Community student, as a kind of golden rule for those at what he called his "stage of life": "to not trust anything too greatly, take everything with a grain of salt…But to be open to listen to everybody and not to shun any opinion." For these adolescents, it seems, there is no greater value than that of keeping an open mind.

Probing the differences between responses

As hinted above, while our interviewees shared a similar preference for making up their own minds about all things, including Israel, behind this similarity lay a profound difference. In the community schools, the students' tendency to search out their own answers transmuted into a pervasive skepticism about their schools' purposes and practices. Such skepticism may not just relate to Israel education but to all aspects of school life. In the Orthodox schools adolescent independence was less likely to be expressed as skepticism of adults, although students still revealed a greater readiness to learn about Israel from peers than from their teachers. Among the students in the community day schools, this tendency was inflected with an expectation of bias among those employed by their schools to teach about Israel, especially so at Kehilati where, as was noted above, students report a strong message of Israel's importance.

In unpacking why it is that students in community schools tend to be so sceptical of their teachers' intentions we can surface important factors behind why Israel education is both so complex and so challenging for such a high proportion of students in the community day school sector.

(a) *A cultural gap:* Paradoxically, a first factor comes into view through analyzing responses among students at Kook, the mid-west modern Orthodox school. In this school, despite repeated pressing by the interviewer, the only students who articulated any sense of conflict or inconsistency between what they heard and observed at school and what they encountered among significant institutions outside schools – families, youth movements and camps – were students who self-identified as *baalei teshuvah*, that is who come from families that had not always been religious, or to be more precise, that were not yet fully socialized into the wider school community. Thus, for almost all Kook students there was an unquestioned plausibility about what they encountered in school. For example, when asked if there was anything that made them embarrassed or ashamed of Israel, their most common response was that Israel needs to do better with its PR in communicating the justice of a cause about which they (and their school) have few doubts.[10]

This comfort with Israel and with the school's relationship to it differed markedly from the response of students in the community schools. In these schools, many interviewees experienced a tension between what they experienced at school

---

10 It is tempting to consider whether greater comfort among the Orthodox students for their schools' position also reflects norms in the Orthodox community that place a much heavier emphasis on the teacher as an authority figure.

and what they encountered in other parts of their lives, at home, in public discourse about Israel in their local community, or in what they learned about Israel from the media. At one level, the divergent messages that come from these other contexts means that students are less willing to be convinced by what they hear at school, but, more fundamentally, the problem for these students is that they are less able or ready to locate themselves within their school's culture - of which, as shown earlier, they have a fairly consistent sense - especially when they might feel more comfortable in other non-school contexts. Thus, at Kehilati a number of students who defined themselves as not being religious found themselves alienated by what they perceived as the school's conviction that a connection to Israel is grounded above all in a set of particular religious beliefs.

A vivid example of such thinking was provided by Michelle from Kehilati, someone whose Jewish father "doesn't," in her own revealing words, "have any religious connection and therefore any potential special connection to Israel" and whose deceased mother wasn't Jewish. Michelle described herself as someone who didn't "feel personally or religiously connected to Israel" and who didn't think that "just because you're a certain religion you have a right to any part of the world." She contrasted the school's belief that "Israel and Judaism are strongly connected" with Habonim camp where "they don't tend to focus on the religious-Israeli connection". The school, she indicates, has not sufficiently demonstrated, after 11 years, how a connection to Israel can be meaningful for a non-religious Jew like her. It seems that the same can be said for her many years in Habonim camp given her jarring admission that "I feel the same connection to Israel as I do to, say, Greenland."[11]

---

11 Michelle's comments are especially jarring given that, historically, Habonim Dror has been constituted as a Labor Zionist Youth Movement. Probed about her disinterest despite attending such an ideologically oriented camp, Michelle explained that she had been drawn to the camp by its socialist orientation, not its Zionism.

(b) *A sense of imbalance*: A second factor feeding student skepticism is a feeling articulated by a number of interviewees that the range (what many interviewees called the "spectrum") of opinions they encounter in school does not properly reflect what they perceive as the true diversity of the student body. This is, first, a complaint about the narrow range of views to which students are exposed by schools, both in the classroom and on school trips to Israel, but it is also a comment on the relative homogeneity of views that students themselves feel comfortable expressing in a day school context, even when, as in Community, there is a deep and consistent affirmation of students' right to be different. A number of interviewees contrasted this homogeneity with the range of opinion they encountered in Jewish summer camps. Ironically, although camps are often more ideologically driven than schools, they are not suspect in these terms (for example, no mention was made of their bias) because most young people participate in their programs in a fully voluntary fashion – something that cannot be said for school, or at least for some of the courses at school that students are required to take.

Dana, a Kehilati student, referenced many of these issues by contrasting the atmosphere in school with that at BBYO, a venue not exactly known for its political intensity, but that evidently she perceived to be much more open than her school.

There's such a different spectrum of opinions, especially because here in a small little private school, it's very much like we're in a bubble. But then once I get into BBYO, these kids are all over the spectrum. Some kids are very pro-Palestinian, some are very pro-Israel and it's a great place to discuss our opinions because here, while we can discuss our opinions, it's always kind of like – we know the teachers are biased. They won't be teaching an Israel class if they weren't. ... I know in my class we'll discuss the Israeli side, we'll discuss the Arab side, but then our teachers will explain why the Arab side isn't necessarily right, and I feel like they could do that for the Israeli side too, but they don't. And that's…frustrating because I don't necessarily think that they should be teaching us in such a biased way.

Many community day school students remarked on the imbalanced nature of what they heard in schools. As Emily, a Kehilati student states: "They don't really portray Israel as a country that does things wrong". Unexpectedly, this criticism was often made by students who were among the most passionate about Israel – perhaps because they were uncomfortable with their convictions being so heavy-handedly promoted by the adult world. Most dramatic in this respect was Mike, a Kehilati student, who attributed his strong pro-Israel convictions to having been "plugged into the propaganda machine" at school, and to having been "spoon-fed" the same messages since he was in kindergarten, something about which he now did not feel comfortable.

As far as one can tell from observations and from interviews with teachers, these schools may in fact be exposing students to multiple perspectives about Israel. Student responses suggest, however, that these efforts are either seen as tokenistic (as one thoughtful student put it, "I *think* they respect other people's views, but I don't think you'd know it if you were here") or as lacking in robustness. This latter critique echoes one made by Hyman in her doctoral dissertation when comparing what she called the "china shop" sensibilities of Jewish studies in liberal day schools with the "jungle gym" atmosphere in general studies (Hyman, 2008). Schools seem to treat matters of Jewish significance quite gingerly for fear of upsetting stakeholders or perhaps of alienating students, but in so doing they may undermine their own purposes by not subjecting important Jewish ideas to the same intensity of critique that is commonplace in other areas of the curriculum.

(c) *Excessive?* A last factor that contributes to the skepticism of community day school students is revealed by the complaint made by some interviewees that their schools are trying too hard to cultivate a commitment to Israel, even while these same interviewees indicate understanding why their schools might be so proactive. Jeremy, a student at Community put it like this: "I know the school really loves Israel, but it just gets redundant; it's always being thrown in your face. At some point, it just gets annoying. It's not because people dislike Israel. It's just like they're sick of hearing about it." On the other side of the country, Jonny, a Kehilati student, used similar language: "I fully understand that the school would want to be pushing forward that view...the love of Israel...I personally would prefer not to be kind of having that thrown in my face all the time."

There are good reasons for taking this criticism seriously but not necessarily for treating it as an objective assessment of the reality. First, in Community and Kehilati, the schools where these complaints were heard, there were also other interviewees who felt that their schools were not doing enough to promote Israel. Emily, a Kehilati student, complained: "I mean, I love Israel so much, and I feel like the school doesn't, except for on *Yom Ha'aztmaut* when the whole school is together singing and dancing and like saying how much they love Israel. Other than that, the focus is more on general studies." Over at Community, Davida felt the same way, remarking how given the diversity of students in the school, it is disappointing that the schools doesn't do "a good enough job to even try and influence their opinions of Israel." A second reason to question the validity of the students' complaints comes from a comparison with the interviewees from Orthodox schools where it is noticeable that none complained about their schools doing too much to promote Israel. In these places we only found students who complained that their schools weren't doing enough. We suspect then that the common complaint in community schools about overdoing Israel education is less important for what it reveals about the intensity of what the schools do; a conclusion that is at best open to question given how different are the emphases even within this subset of schools, as the students from Community and Kehilati themselves indicate. Complaints about excessiveness are probably more important for what they reveal about the mind-set of students and what schools may not have done to take account of such thinking.

Conclusion

Undoubtedly, community day schools face a special challenge in engaging the commitments and interests of an unusually wide range of students – a range that in Jewish terms may be wider than has perhaps ever before been experienced by full-time Jewish educational institutions. Those who lead these institutions may not have sufficiently considered how little of what they, as educators, take for granted about Israel is shared by their students. Families and young people are motivated by a wide range of reasons to enroll in Jewish day school; receiving a Jewish or Israel orientated education is not a primary consideration for many. Evidently, therefore, students do not readily understand why schools devote so much time to Israel-related events over the course of the year, why the study of Hebrew is compulsory but not the study of other second languages, and why one might view Israel as integral to any understanding of what it means to be Jewish in America. What was self-understood for one generation needs today to be justified in an age-appropriate fashion that takes special account of adolescent suspicion of people who, in the words of one interviewee, "are clearly biased and trying to convince you of something."

It is no wonder that student skepticism in community day schools about what they perceive as their schools' agenda to promote or defend Israel contrasts so sharply with how interviewees from Orthodox schools talk. Skepticism is fueled by a disconnect between school culture and the values that derive from significant institutions outside school, by what is perceived as a lack of robustness in how schools handle Israel, and by an unfamiliarity with some of the basic reasons why adults in their schools regard Israel as so important for Jews living in America. In Orthodox schools, by contrast, there is much greater cultural coherence between the different contexts within which students lead their lives especially in the nexus between school, home and camp. In such an environment, Israel's centrality in Jewish life is taken for granted.

Evidently, even as schools have become ever more creative in their delivery of Israel education, and while some have been ready to recognize and embrace what makes a relationship with Israel complex, they may have still taken too much for granted about their students and the starting points from which they enter a relationship with Israel. There is a lot to be said for listening closely to how these young people make sense of the world and of Israel's place within it.

NOTES FOR EDUCATORS ON
COMPLICATING ISRAEL

Complicating Israel is perhaps the most contested domain of Israel education today. Educators hotly debate questions around this issue: When and how, developmentally speaking, is it appropriate to introduce complexity into the teaching of Israel? At what point might complicating Israel interfere or prevent cultivation of feelings of attachment and desire to engage? What is the right balance between grounding learners in core narratives and allowing for critical inquiry and personal meaning making around the place of Israel in Jewish life? Many also ask a more personal question: How can I complicate Israel when I myself don't understand so much of what is going on?

In various ways the vignettes in this section challenge us to consider these questions carefully in terms of background, levels of Jewish engagement, and the social and emotional context of learners today. The first three vignettes describe approaches to Israel education that we define as critical engagement, a deep exploration of the multiple and complex dimensions of Israel as a Land, People, and State. Vignette 1 sets the stage by first examining some of the complexity in the relationship between the words Israel, Nation, and People, especially as they play out in contemporary Israeli society. It then turns to experiences that many HUC students confront during their first year of studies in Israel that impact on their relationship and connections to each of these dimensions of Land, People, and State. Their experiences and interactions with Israel and Israelis often raise critical questions about Jewish belonging, democratic values, and the relationship between religion and state. Vignette 2 then explores some of the educational processes that allow these students both to study these questions in-depth and grapple with them on an intellectual, emotional, and spiritual level.

Vignettes 3 and 4 look at complicating Israel in Jewish high schools. The first of these describes the attempt at one community day school to offer 12th grade students the opportunity to engage with a rich array of historical, sociological, and cultural sources to explore some of the complexities of Israeli society in general and the Israel-Palestinian conflict in particular. Consistent with the schools broad educational goals, their goals for teaching Israel are to help their students develop their own understandings of what Israel means to them, rather than inducting them into a particular ideological stance towards Israel. As we see in Vignette 4, the risk of an educational institution providing a singular answer to the question "Why Israel matters" without providing students an opportunity to really explore what the question means, can lead to skepticism and mistrust, particularly in liberal settings.

These vignettes show that complicating Israel is difficult. It takes a clear sense of purpose, clearly articulated goals that allow for students to develop their own stance and relationship to Israel rather than accepting a tacit or explicit "party line." Vignette 4 in particular, is consistent with another study of "value tensions" around Israel in a community day school (Zakai, 2011) that also shows that mixed messages about educational goals towards Israel can lead to mistrust and distance.

Complicating Israel requires educators who are steeped in Israel education and can present a rich array of historical, sociological, and cultural materials to their students. Complicating also requires extensive use of primary sources and avoiding a frontal approach to imparting information, focusing instead on holistic and relational learning where no question is out of bounds and dialogue is stressed over doctrine. In applying these principles, even in a program with a distinctly ideological slant, a teacher would create curriculum that left room for more conversation, questions, and opportunities to reflect on what all of this means to the individual learners. The learning that takes place in such settings does not focus on espousal of or adherence to correct points of view. Rather, it is designed to open learners up to multiple possibilities for interpretation and construction of personal meaning.

Theoretical groundings for putting "complicating" into practice

Similar to the principle of integration, a complicated approach to Israel education can be connected to the tradition of progressive education that began with John Dewey in the early 20th century. Dewey advocated an educational system that functioned both in balance with and in tension between the learner and the subject matter that the community determines the learner needs to know. Dewey understood the value of learning about the past to better understand the present and the value of simultaneously embracing tradition while developing the capacity for critical thinking and personal autonomy.

Much of Dewey's thinking is consonant with more contemporary theories of constructivist learning which emerged out of the fields of developmental and cognitive psychology. Like Dewey, constructivist theory presumes that knowledge is socially constructed by the individual learner through a process of shared interaction and experience. Also like Dewey, constructivism maintains that knowledge is useful only when it has effect. Such an approach argues that learning is a reciprocal process of cultural transmission, whereby individuals shape and are shaped by their cultural context. They construct their own understanding by integrating, synthesizing, and testing the stimuli they receive to build upon, and sometimes reshape existing frameworks or meaning schemes. It is congruent with contemporary theory in adult education that suggests that the educator's primary goal is to foster a change in the learner's way of viewing or organizing the world.

There are a number of tools and techniques that are generally associated with constructivist theory. Such an approach focuses on empowering the learner by facilitating self-directed learning, developing critical thinkers, and the dialogic nature of change. It utilizes the past to gain insight about the present. It emphasizes questions over answers, encourages cooperative rather than individual learning, and maintains a balanced focus on the learners' present needs and future potential.

Applying these tools and techniques to teaching Israel can create an environment that allows learners to make their own meaning, to tolerate ambiguity, and to think critically about given facts and accepted truths. Rather than advocating the formation of certain kinds of "correct" beliefs, values, and behaviors, Israel education consonant with constructivist theory enables and provokes learners to challenge, shape, and strengthen their own beliefs, values, and behaviors. Rather than providing singular answers, Israel educators ask multiple questions and encourage learners to think things through for themselves.

Translating these ideas into practice requires educators who provide their learners with clear messages about the orientation and expectations of the learning experience. Ideally, such teaching would simultaneously give learners a sense of connection to a master story that has sacred significance and also leave room for questions, uncertainty, and multiple interpretations. Indeed, an essential task of religious education of any kind should be to help individuals learn to live with paradox by balancing the tensions of the apparent contradictions of life (Brennan, 1980). While the balancing act is the learner's job, the educational context and structure can provide secure scaffolding upon which to climb.

Israel educators also must be sensitive to group dynamics and individual learning styles to determine just what educational technique will work best in what circumstance. Content teaching must be interwoven with questions such as: "What does this site, text, story or experience mean to me?"; "What are its implications for my religious beliefs and practice?"; and "How might it enrich my life as a member of the American Jewish community?"

Perhaps the most sophisticated skill entails developing an awareness of how much ambiguity the learners can tolerate. It requires knowing when to provoke and when to appease, when to tell a story and when to ask the participants to find their own stories in the landscape, texts, news reports, cultural artifacts, and encounters they will read about, experience, and meet. It requires a teacher who can make formal and informal linkages between time and space, between history and memory, between Jewish practice and Jewish identity. It requires what Donald Schön (1995) calls "reflection in action," the sensitivity to know when to ask questions and when to offer blessings, to know when to talk about why does *Torah* come from Zion and when to talk about the aspirations and shortcomings of a Jewish and democratic state, to show that heaven does indeed touch earth and both are essential to one's relationship to Israel and Jewish life.

Recent research on the teaching of Israel in American Jewish educational settings suggests that we are still far from achieving the goal of teaching Israel as a complex, multi-textured, and integral aspect of Jewish life. A study of the teaching of Israel in Reform congregations shows the goal of connecting Israel to Reform Jewish life is mentioned about half as often as the more vague and diffuse goal of "creating a positive attitude towards Israel" (Grant, 2007). Likewise, Pomson's and Dietcher's (2010) research on Israel education in American Jewish day schools across the denominational spectrum suggests that attitudinal goals are more important than cognitive or behavioral ones. In other words, educators appear more concerned with "encouraging young people to be concerned with and about Israel" than they are with students gaining knowledge or understanding that is meaningful and relevant to each individual student (p. 58).

As such, Israel education in many day schools more closely resembles Israel advocacy, with reliance on materials prepared to help students "combat" anti-Israel rhetoric on university campuses. The Israel advocacy curriculum tends to continue a tradition of viewing Israel in mythical terms, an ideal society with which to express solidarity and defend. In contrast, in a situation of mature love, the individual is able to grapple with a deep understanding and complex relationship that includes an understanding that the other (in this case Israel) is not perfect. Nevertheless, the other is an important part of one's life, so important in fact that successful Israel education enables the student to develop critical opinions and political positions about how Israel's state and society can better reflect the values in which they believe. As in life, critical engagement breeds a mature, stable love which understands that life is not perfect and the other will not always be like me. Nevertheless, we are tied to each based on the bonds of common history, perceptions of shared fate and mutual interests, and the desire to build a future together.

A growing consensus towards complicating

Despite the continuing tendency to treat Israel as a mythological other and the dominance of Israel advocacy as the primary educational tool utilized by American Jews, we do see a shifting tide in attitudes towards complicating Israel among some scholars, teachers, and policy leaders. Evidence of this move is documented regularly in the Jewish Press.[12] More substantively, evidence is also reflected in a number of professional development and curricular initiatives that recognize that oversimplified and uni-dimensional approaches to teaching Israel are inadequate. These initiatives are designed to deepen educators' knowledge about the multiple dimensions of Israeli history, culture, politics, religion, and society. They seem to be striving to provide greater knowledge and interpretative tools necessary to shape understandings of issues such as army incursions into Gaza, intra-religious tensions, the status of Jewish and non-Jewish minority groups such as Ethiopians and Arab citizens of Israel, and the relationship between the Jewish People and the Jewish State.

Among those most compatible with our idea to complicate Israel as described by these vignettes, are the iCenter, the Shalom

---

12 For example articles in The Jewish Week such as "New Consensus Seen Emerging in Israel Education (Wiener, Julie, December 7, 2010), "Day Schools Need New Israel Ed Approach" (Rosenblatt, Gary, February 16, 2011), "We've Got it Backward: Israel Education Should Come First, Then Advocacy (Gary Rosenblatt, July 19, 2011).

Hartman Institute's "Engaging Israel" initiative, Makom: The Israel Engagement Network of the Jewish Agency, and the Center for Israel Education (CIE) in partnership with the Emory Institute for Modern Israel. Each of these organizations take a rigorous approach to advancing the field of Israel education by providing high quality and academically sound resources for use by rabbis, educators, and lay audiences.

The iCenter, founded in 2009, recently published a document called the Aleph-Bet of Israel Education that provides a comprehensive framework for thinking about and doing Israel education in the 21st century. This model is grounded in the belief that Israel education must be related to Jewish identity development. This starting point is aligned with our foundational premise that Israel education must be seen as an integral part of Jewish life. The iCenter's work focuses on creating educational processes and experiences that will lead to "generations of young North American Jews for whom contemporary Israel is an integral and vibrant part of their personal and collective Jewish identity". The iCenter is also taking the lead in pioneering the creation of a certificate in Israel education in partnership with six institutions of higher education that offer master's degrees in Jewish education, with the expressed goal of preparing "*1,000 skilled, certified and employed Israel educators for the field by 2020*" (iCenter, 2012).

Likewise, the Shalom Hartman Institute's Engaging Israel program reflects Israel education as we understand it, as described in the following statement:

Now is the time to invite Jews from around the world to engage in thinking about the meaning that Israel can have in their lives and how they can be enriched and positively influenced by the reality of a Jewish Nation.[13]

Their program utilizes a combination of videotaped lectures by scholars and experts in Jewish studies, Middle East politics and history along with discussion texts and other web resources that

---

13 Quote from the Shalom Hartman Institute Website, April 2012.

congregations and other Jewish institutions can use to enrich their adult education offerings.

Makom describes its work as embracing "the vibrant complexity of Israel: the People and the Place. We create content and cultivate Jewish activists, educators, rabbis, arts and community leaders to develop sophisticated and honest programs that spark and forge commitment."[14]   They are involved in a wide range of activities including development of curricular resources, consultation with communities, and program development for targeted audiences such as post-Birthright participants on college campuses. They also consult on Israel travel and serve as a clearinghouse for educational and cultural resources.

Finally, another important educational initiative is the Center for Israel Education (CIE) that both writes curriculum about modern Israel and offers professional development workshops, school consultations, and seminars for pre-collegiate level educators. CIE Director Kenneth Stein (2009) describes the goal is to "witness history as it unfolded, not as it is concluded" (p.12). The approach to historical analysis of "big issues" and "big questions" relies largely on primary documents and academic scholarship. As Stein writes: "When learners are offered a window through which to glimpse history, as it actually happened, they better contextualize the situations and perspectives of the time. Primary sources offer this critical perspective" (p. 12).

Curricular Materials

Educators often look for prepared curriculum to use in teaching. Of course, such materials are important resources, but they are hardly the sole answer to the challenge of teaching any subject matter, including Israel. Curriculum is inherently ideological in that the content, methods, visuals, and other materials used are grounded in values that may or may not cohere with the educator's goals, whether articulated or not.

---

14 Quote from the Makom website, March 2012.

The ideological orientation of Israel curriculum was made evident by a recent project undertaken at the Melton Centre for Jewish Education at the Hebrew University. This analysis of a range of sources, including denominational movements, commercial publishers, and independent organizations, shows the diversity of approaches that can be found in these prepared materials. The Melton Centre team developed a classification system for Israel curriculum according to six different "orientations": a Classical Zionist model, an Israel engagement model, a Jewish Peoplehood model, a Romantic/Realist model, the classical Jewish text model, and a Visionary model (Isaacs, 2011).

Simply delineating such categories reveals that what was in earlier years the standard underlying assumption of Israel as the center of Jewish life and the Diaspora as the periphery, no longer is the singular organizing model for Jewish life. It now appears that there are numerous goals and approaches for the teaching of Israel, whether or not they are explicitly revealed by the curriculum authors. Each of these approaches tells a different story and each, either implicitly or explicitly conveys a different set of values and expected commitments to be made. Thus, curriculum users need to be careful consumers in order to determine whether the underlying values of the materials are indeed consistent with the approach they wish to take.

Examples of recent curriculum that attempt to confront more of the complexities in Israeli society include materials created for eighth grade students in congregational schools by the Melton Center for Jewish Education at the Jewish Theological Seminary. Titled, *Israel Today: Realizing the Dream* it introduces a host of social challenges including the divide between Orthodox and secular Jews, the status of Arabs with Israeli citizenship, problems of poverty, the plight of foreign workers in Israel, the Palestinian conflict, and tensions between Orthodox and non-Orthodox religious Jews. As Rabbi Shelley Kniaz, the primary writer of the Melton Center curriculum said, "Doing the oranges and Hasidim approach that you get in pre-school and that unfortunately lasts all through their synagogue education just is not going to fly. We are in trouble if people can't love the real Israel. If we can't love Israel the way she is, it's taking the rug out of any connection with Israel the State".[15]

Another example is *Artzeinu: An Israel Encounter* (Grishaver & Barkin, 2008), a curriculum intended for upper elementary grades in congregational schools. On its opening pages, this curriculum reveals it will also explore societal challenges, including inter and intra-religious strife. In a paragraph that begins with the birth of the modern state of Israel, the authors write: "Israel, a Hebrew-speaking nation that struggles with how religious and non-religious live together, with how Jew and non-Jew share a Jewish State, that has lots of problems and lots of opportunities, has become a Jewish Homeland" (p. 1).

The richness of any educational experience often lies in its complexity. If educators truly hope to help learners expand the depth of their understanding about how Israel and Judaism intersect, then the learning process must risk introducing dissonance and disequilibrium in order to recast and reframe meaning. This is far more difficult to do while remaining comfortably ensconced in the realm of myth and symbol. It requires entering into the more problematic and troublesome issues of modern life in a modern Jewish State. It is in this tension where the creative spark and the opportunities for transformation lie.

Thus, grappling with representations of the ideal and real Israel together, as complementary rather than oppositional points of view, creates the learning moment. Managing the apparent contradictions between these multiple images of Israel and Judaism makes it possible to both preserve and challenge meaning systems. It helps people feel grounded in both master stories and modern sensibilities. It allows for both critical thinking and shared community. It teaches people to be comfortable in seeking questions, not answers. It helps them to recognize their inherent biases and allows them to see another

---

15 Telephone interview, November 19, 2008.

point of view, without losing and hopefully even enriching their personal sense of meaning. Perhaps most significantly, it keeps Israel a dynamic force in their lives, no matter how distant the separation in time and space. And, if these dynamic dimensions of Israel can be integrated into what it means to be Jewish, then Israel can retain a place in American Jewish life.

III. CONNECT: BUILDING SOCIAL NETWORKS BETWEEN JEWS INSIDE AND OUTSIDE OF ISRAEL

Israel education is an essential component of a Jewish education that nurtures an individual's connection to collective Jewish understanding and experience. Thus, Israel education must focus on the point where individuals meet the group. Successful Israel Education promotes a broad sense of collective Jewish belonging, which is generated through a combination of two points at which individuals connect to a group: Through (1) symbolic actions; and (2) social, interpersonal connections. This section of our book focuses on how the symbolic and social forms of Israel education mix.

Symbolic actions

In terms of educational priority, symbolic actions (which are rooted in ceremony, ritual and celebratory events) come first, as they promote an emotional connection between an individual and the Jewish People. That emotional connection is the primary building block upon which Jewish education of any type rests. In Israel education, activities which are symbolic in nature connect participants to Israel and Israelis with no expectation that the educational experience will produce actual social relationships. The desired result is what Benedict Anderson (1991) calls the "imagined community," a group whose members might include millions of individuals (or more) spanning large periods of history and disparate geographical areas. Such a group exists because of the ability of its members to imagine their connection to one another, in spite of the fact they may never meet in face-to-face relationships.

Social connections

In contrast, are activities that foster actual social relationships in which the participant comes to feel a concrete sense of obligation to maintain a relationship with either another individual or social group. Here the emphasis is not on the imagined community of millions of people, but rather an obligation to maintain the social relationship with an individual or individuals.

Symbolic + social = excellent Israel education

Until approximately 30 years ago, almost all educational work associated with Israel in Diaspora Jewish communities was grounded in symbolic rather than social connections to Israel. There were two basic types of symbolic activities: 1) ceremonies which centered on Israel Independence Days or events such as parades or demonstrations of solidarity; and 2) knowledge acquisition through formal learning about modern Israeli history with a focus on the founding of the State and Israel's wars.

While the symbolic is a primary building block of Israel education; without the social, Israel remains as something "out there," another world which is not part of everyday life. Fostering social connections between Diaspora and Israeli Jews makes Israel a more personally accessible reality. This social corrective has been slow in coming, but in the past 30 years there has been a steady rise in forms of Israel education that focus on a social orientation, often labeled as "People-to-People (P2P) programming."

People-to-People (P2P) programming

P2P programming involves building connections between individual Jews living inside and outside of Israel, between students, families, teachers, and lay leaders in the partner communities.

The largest framework for P2P Israel-Diaspora relationships is the Jewish Agency's Partnership 2000 that was first established in the mid-1990s. As of 2007, it was running partnerships between 45 regions in Israel with 550 Jewish communities around the world (Arbel, 2010). A central activity pursued by many of the partnerships is school-to-school twinning programs. In the 2009-10 academic year the school twinning programs included 159

Israeli schools with 17,000 Israeli pupils and 211 Diaspora Jewish schools with 11,160 Diaspora pupils and hundreds of educators from both Israel and the Diaspora.[16]

People-to-People type programs also can be found in some congregational schools settings. For example, since 2005 over 30 Reform and Conservative congregational schools have participated in a virtual *mifgash* through a shared curriculum project developed by the Lokey International Academy of Jewish Studies at the Leo Baeck Education Center in Haifa (Grant, 2006). Initially, this project was built around a series of units that include the exchange of work products between two classrooms, one in Israel and the other in the United States. The program would culminate in a video-conference in which the two groups interact in real time. Vignette 3 in this section of the book describes this program in greater detail, including how it has evolved over time.

P2P encounters take place in the adult population as well. For instance, Jewish day school teacher trips to Israel often include some kind of meeting with educators in a sister city (Pomson & Grant, 2004), as do most Federation-sponsored and community trips. In a study of community day schools, Kopelowitz (2005) found that 46% of participating schools encourage their students to participate in activities that promote social engagement with Israel, either through partnership programs, events that create connections to Israeli youth, or (to a much lesser extent) programs that encourage *aliyah*.

Another type of social interaction is evidenced in Jewish communities in Baltimore, Cincinnati, Washington, D.C., Northern New Jersey, and Connecticut (among others) that participate in a young emissary program through the Jewish Agency. Through this program, pairs of Israeli post-high school age young adults spend a year living with families and working in

---

16 These are the numbers provided by Partnership 2000 of the Jewish Agency. These numbers do not include at least another estimated 100 schools engaged in similar programming outside the P2K framework.

schools and other Jewish educational settings in their partnership communities. The families who host these young adults informally report that they are profoundly affected by the experience. They maintain contact with their "adopted" sons and daughters and visit them for years after.

In yet another example, *Ki Va Moed*, a program sponsored by UJA-Federation of New York, four Suffolk County congregations are involved in long term partnering activities and seminars with lay and professional counterparts in seven schools and communities in Israel. This project has been ongoing for several years and program evaluations[17] suggest that it is making a significant difference in the lives of its participants on both sides of the ocean.

The three vignettes in this section each explores a particular aspect of the manner in which successful Israel education uses both symbolic and social connections in order to nurture the connection between individual Jews and the Jewish People.

The first vignette focuses on "the *mifgash*," planned educational encounters between Jews who live inside and outside of Israel. The *mifgash* is perhaps one of the oldest and certainly one of the most central educational strategies utilized by Israel educators who consciously seek to develop social connections between Jews in Israel and the Diaspora. By looking at the historical development of the *mifgash* and delineating its core educational qualities, we gain a broader understanding of the field.

The second vignette looks at the variety of ways in which the presence of Israeli staff at summer camps can serve to develop both the symbolic and social aspects of connecting to Israel. The third vignette provides a case study of a school-to-school twinning initiative that began as a shared curriculum project and has evolved into something more multi-layered and sophisticated.

---

17 This is based on correspondence in September, 2007 with Shellie Dickstein *Ki Va Mo'ed* grant administrator at SAJES, the Suffolk County New York board of Jewish education, and Roberta Bell-Kliger, program evaluator from Oranim College in Tivon, Israel.

VIGNETTE 1: THE MIFGASH

Every field has foundational practices. For Israel education "the *mifgash*" is one such practice. The Hebrew concept of *"mifgash"* (plural, *mifgashim*) refers to a planned educational in-person meeting of Jews who live inside and outside of Israel.

The increasing use of *mifgashim* as an educational strategy is a central part of the broader trend of adding in a social dimension, alongside the symbolic aspects of Israel educational. Prior to the 1990s few trips by Diaspora Jews to Israel included educationally informed interactions with Israeli Jews. The practice of the organized educational encounter gained momentum in 1994 with the creation of *Mifgashim* by the Charles R. Bronfman Foundation, an organization dedicated to furthering the idea of the inter-personal encounter between Israeli and Diaspora Jews as a basic educational tool. *Mifgashim* closed as an independent organization in 2001, but the concept of the *mifgash* had by then taken firm root as a basic component in many of the educational experiences that include Israeli and Diaspora Jews.

Over the past twenty years, *mifgashim* have become a core component of Israel educational travel programs. Today, it is a commonplace assumption among educators involved with educational travel programs to Israel that the successful *mifgash* provides extensive benefit for all participants in the area of Jewish identity development and belonging. Acceptance has reached the point that the Israeli army now gives time off from service to approximately 4,000 active soldiers each year, to travel with their Diaspora counterparts on Birthright buses as full participants for half of the overall trip (Sasson et al., 2008).

Ingredients of a successful mifgash

Despite the now wide-spread assumption that the *mifgash* brings educational benefits, the research that we discuss in this and the other vignettes points to the fact that not all *mifgashim* are equal. Some bring greater benefit than others. Indeed, in some cases a poorly executed *mifgash* can actually lead participants to reinforce their negative stereotypes or even develop new ones.

The *mifgash* philosophy is predicated on the understanding that educational benefits accrue to both the Israeli and non-Israeli participants, and the broader communities in which they live. A successful *mifgash* leads to an overall increase in awareness of the power and meaning of Jewish collective experience for all involved parties. Ongoing, sustained *mifgashim* have the further potential to generate "Peoplehood consciousness," defined by Kopelowitz and Ravid (2010) as a "generalized sense of commitment to the Jewish People and its civilization, which extends over and above the immediate social encounter with other Jews" (p. 10).

Prior research on *mifgashim* between Israeli and Diaspora Jews on the Israel experience (Bar-Shalom, 1998; Feldman & Katz, 2002) and in summer camps (Bram & Neria, 2003b) demonstrates that if certain conditions are not met, the encounter can bring about the unintended consequence of strengthening negative stereotypes of the "other" and hence educational failure. Yet, research on *mifgashim* also tells us that under favorable conditions, the encounter has the potential to reduce stereotypes and bring about positive change in one's perception of the "other". A positive *mifgash* experience enables group members to see the other groups as more similar to their own group (Horenczyk & Bekerman, 1997; Kujawski, 2000; Sasson et al., 2008; Wolf, 2007). Furthermore, the *mifgash* allows participants in both groups to broaden their understanding of Jewish Peoplehood, as they make sense of the similarities and differences between themselves and the members of the other group (Bar-Shalom, 1998; Ezrachi, 1994).

The best of contemporary *mifgashim* go beyond their original focus on providing an opportunity for Diaspora and Israeli Jews to meet. *Mifgashim* are increasingly designed to enable participants to explore Jewish culture and communal settings different from their own, through educational travel that includes contact with other Jews as a central element. Today, many Israeli participants travel to Diaspora communities[18] and often American, Israeli, and Jews from countries other than Israel travel together to a range of sites in Europe, North Africa, and elsewhere.

The Tri-Center project, run by the World Confederation of Jewish Community Centers (WCJCC) is an example of an exemplary *mifgash* experience. The goal of the project is to develop a sense of *Klal Yisrael* by creating a working relationship between Jewish Community Centers from three different communities, one in Israel, one in North America, and the third from another part of the Jewish world. A central focus of the project is the development of inter-personal relationships between teens, young adults, and the lay and professional leadership from the three communities through a series of *mifgashim* in each of the participating communities (Kopelowitz, 2010b).

One of the foundational beliefs of the iCenter, founded in 2009, is that the *mifgash* is a platform for Jewish education beyond the Israel travel experience itself.[19] The organization seeks to promote the *mifgash* as an integral component for Jewish education in general, both in the context of Israel trips, and also between Jews in other contexts.

The ingredients that contribute to a successful *mifgash* provide a looking glass into core practices of People-to-People programming. The success of a *mifgash* depends on close collaboration between sponsoring organizations to the point where program participants fully integrate and become a single experiential group during the encounter. Such planning requires a focus on the smallest details. For example, Birthright mandates that when Israeli soldiers join a Birthright bus, they sit next to

---

18 For a similar argument see Mittelberg,2011. For a focused case study of the Mifgash in the context of American Jewish summer camps see: Wolf & Kopelowitz, 2003. There is a relatively large literature on Mifgashim; see, for example: Feldman & Katz, 2002; Kopelowitz, 2003; Wolf, 2007.
19 http://www.theicenter.org/

Lisa Grant and Ezra Kopelowitz

non-Israelis and not with one another. The result is integration of participants into a single group on the bus, and not "the Israelis" and the "non-Israelis" sitting as two separate groups. In another example, one summer camp director makes sure that Israeli counselors (also known as *shlichim*) do not eat, sleep, vacation and work separately from the American counselors, which is the more typical case in many Jewish summer camps (Wolf & Kopelowitz, 2003).

A *mifgash* transcends the immediate social experience of the encounter and produces Peoplehood consciousness when three conditions are in place:

1.   Creation of a social experience of Peoplehood

The *mifgash* is an intense and enjoyable social interaction with Jews who are different from oneself.

2.   Facilitation of a continued Jewish journey

The program is designed to encourage and enable continued social contact between participants, and,

3.   Building intellectual understandings and emotional connections that strengthen a sense of collective Jewish belonging

A successful *mifgash* facilitates an understanding and awareness among participants that the relationship benefits them both as individuals, and as Jews who are members of a broader Jewish collective. That realization can foster an initial commitment both to one's personal Jewish journey and to contributing to the community (local and global) where that journey unfolds.

In most *mifgashim*, only the first of these three conditions are met. One example, in which all three conditions are met, at least in terms of program design, occurs in the more sophisticated of the school twinning programs, such as the Boston-Haifa partnership (Mittelberg, 2011) which is overseen by the Department of Jewish Peoplehood–Oren, of the Shdemot Center for

Community Leadership at Oranim Academic College. The twinning program rests on creating concentric circles of engagement between communities. It begins by matching communities and schools. Within each school community, the primary targets are those directly involved with the program, the students, their educators, and involved administrators. However, for long lasting impact to occur the mifgash necessarily involves wider circles including parents, other students, educators, administrators, the school's lay leadership, and others involved in the educational life of the wider community. The result is on-going contact between the school communities and a deep and lasting impact (in theory – no longitudinal research exists) on educators and policy makers (Brochstein & Bell Kligler, 2008).

In summary, a look at successful a *mifgash* practice, provides a window into the educational logic and benefits of developing social connections between Diaspora and Israeli Jews. The most sophisticated of the *mifgashim* not only strengthen the Jewish identity of the participants, but also benefit their educational organizations and communities, creating Jewish collective belonging in practice. For this reason, Israel education in general, and the *mifgash* in particular, should be a central element of the educational tool kit used by Jewish educators and community builders today.

VIGNETTE 2: PEOPLE-TO-PEOPLE STRATEGIES FOR ISRAEL EDUCATION AT SUMMER CAMP

As we have noted, American Jewish educational institutions have long emphasized the symbolic importance of Israel. Indeed, one may enter most Jewish institutions (educational or not) in the Diaspora today and immediately notice symbolic associations with Israel, from pictures on the wall, newspapers on a table, and music playing. An equally present part of many Jewish institutions are Israeli staff, either those who no longer live in Israel or those who are visiting. As part of the move towards integrating a social dimension, to complement the symbolic, the most sophisticated educational organizations are now making more explicit use of Israeli staff with the goal of developing the social connection of their staff and students to Israel. In the first vignette of the integrate section, we saw an example of schools that brought their Israeli Hebrew teachers and American Judaic Studies teachers to collaborate in planning their Israel trip. In this vignette, we explore this same phenomenon in the context of Jewish summer camping.

Israel is a central part of the educational experience at most Jewish summer camps (Cohen & Melchior, 2011; Sales, Samuel & Boxer, 2011). The presence of Israel can include the use of Israeli locations to name buildings, the use of spoken Hebrew, Israeli music, food, and Israel day. In the final vignette of the book we take an in-depth look at the evolving nature of Israel education in one camp. In this vignette we focus on the manner in which camp educators might make conscious use of the social connections that develop between Israeli staff, American counselors, and campers.

What is the role of an Israeli staff member in an American Jewish summer camp? This question was posed as part of a research project conducted in 2003 for the Department of Jewish Zionist Education of the Jewish Agency (Wolf & Kopelowitz, 2003). The project used summer camps as a case study for work being done at the Jewish Agency at that time to understand the educational implications of changes taking place in the relationship between Jews in Israel and the Diaspora (Bar-Shalom, 2003; Kopelowitz, 2003).

In 2003 the Jewish Agency summer camp program sent approximately 1,200 Israeli staff with the explicit mission of "bringing Israel" to the camps (Bram & Neria, 2003a, 2003b; Neria, 2003). That number has increased to 1700 by 2011.[20]   Up until approximately 2002, the mission of the Israeli staff, also referred to by the Jewish Agency staff as *shlichim* (emissaries), in the American camp was straightforward. The role of the *shaliach* was to *represent* Israel to Diaspora Jewry. Successful educational work meant convincing Diaspora Jews to make *aliyah* (immigrate) to Israel. If immigration was not possible, then the next mission was to strengthen the connection of Diaspora Jews with the Jewish Homeland. In this "Classical Zionist" paradigm, the educational mission is located solely in the Diaspora. The Jewish and Zionist identity of the Israeli Jew is taken for granted. The significant change at the Jewish Agency in 2003 was the idea that the Israeli counselors themselves are a target of the educational mission of the *shlichut* program. If the summer camp work is successful, then beyond strengthening the Jewish and Zionist identities of Diaspora Jews, the taken for granted values that counselors bring to their work are also challenged and strengthened.

What types of social and educational interactions between the Israeli and Americans must occur in order for both to undergo a transformative identity experience? What policies must be pursued in order to create work conditions that will enable Israeli staff, both to bring Israel to the summer camp, and at the same time to undergo a transformative Jewish-Zionist experience themselves?   To answer these questions Wolf and Kopelowitz (2003) interviewed summer camp directors. The directors are key actors in the world of summer camps and in any change process that the Jewish Agency might seek to implement.

---

20. Jewish Agency website.

The Research

The research conducted by Wolf and Kopelowitz did not seek a representative picture of the way all summer camp directors think, but rather, to describe the work of directors with different approaches to the question of Israeli staff in American camps. With this goal in mind, they created a small and extremely focused sample of seven directors of Jewish summer camps in North America. The directors were selected with the help of the director of the Summer Camp Program at the Jewish Agency with the goal of creating a sample of movement and organization[21] based camps that he felt represented a variety of approaches towards the Israeli *shlichim*. The interviews included directors from two Ramah (Conservative movement) camps, two URJ (Reform movement) camps, two JCC (Jewish Community Center) camps, and one Young Judea camp. Some of the directors included in this sample were known to regard Israeli staff as important to the life and ideology of their camp, and invest a relatively large amount of time trying to make the work experience of the *shlichim* successful. In other words, an effort was made to find directors who were serious about Israel and Israelis in their camps, yet pursued very different strategies vis-à-vis the question at hand. Each director was interviewed in person or by phone[22].

Three Strategies vis-à-vis the Work of Israeli Summer Camp Staff

The interviews revealed three distinct approaches of the directors towards Israeli staff in their camps. To understand the

---

21. Movement based camps are those affiliated with different Jewish religious streams, in this case, the Reform and Conservative movements. In regards to organization-based camps, we mean camps affiliated with particular Jewish or Zionist organizations, in this case, the Jewish Community Center Association (JCCA) and Young Judaea.

[22] The findings of similar study focusing at the level of *shilchim* working at a single camp resonate closely to this research. For more information see: Alex Sinclair. 2009. "A New Heuristic Device for the Analysis of Israel Education: Observations from a Jewish Summer Camp." *Journal of Jewish Education*, 75:1, pp. 79-106.

approaches, Wolf and Kopelowitz introduce two sets of concepts and then offer a detailed description of each of the three approaches as seen through the eyes of the summer camp directors.

1. Integration vs. Separation

The first set of concepts revolves around directors who strive for a *functional separation* of the Israeli staff from the camp community versus directors who view *functional integration* of the Israeli staff as their ideal. For those who emphasize separation, the Israeli staff tends to work only as specialists (e.g., Hebrew teachers, nature instructors), and often eat and/or sleep separately from the campers. The involvement of the Israelis in the planning and implementation of camp-wide activities generally focuses on Israel-specific programs, which they tend to plan as a separate organized group (*mishlachat*), rather than in partnership with non-Israeli staff. *Shlichim* in functionally separate camps also tend to socialize among themselves, tending to spend their days off and free-time as a group.

In contrast, the directors who emphasize integration have the Israelis working as cabin counselors (*madrichim*), division heads, and as specialists. In many cases, they sleep in the cabins with the campers and often eat at camper tables. Though much of the Israeli involvement in planning and implementation of camp-wide activities also tends to focus on Israel-related programs, they do so in partnership with non-Israeli staff. Furthermore, the Israeli counselors are encouraged to get involved in planning programs unrelated to Israel. In functionally integrated camps, *shlichim* also tend to socialize with non-Israeli staff during free time and days off.

2. Representative vs. Interpersonal

The second distinction between directors is between those who highlight the *representative value* of the counselor, qua Israeli, in the camp versus those who are interested in the educational payoff of the *interpersonal interactions* between Israelis and Americans in the everyday life of the camp.

The directors who view the Israelis as representatives see them as representing "Israel" and "Israelis," in both a real and symbolic sense to the campers. The Israeli staff makes palpable for the camper what is otherwise a distant reality, bringing a specific educational style, ways of behavior and the spoken Hebrew language to the camp. Beyond their day-to-day responsibilities, the Israelis are encouraged to invest time in planning camp-wide events that are rich in symbolic value, such as an Israel Day celebration or a commemoration ceremony for victims of terrorist attacks. The goal of these events is to emphasize the symbolic importance of Israel in the life of the camp, an act that is enhanced by the involvement of Israeli staff in running the events.

In contrast, the directors who emphasize the interpersonal dimension focus on the ability of the Israeli staff to connect at the emotional level with campers and other staff in the course of everyday life. Through the "little moments" as opposed to larger symbolic events, the directors expect members of the camp community to learn about Israel.

Three Strategies

In combination, the integration/separation and representation/personalization distinctions enable Wolf and Kopelowitz to place the directors on a spectrum with two end points and a middle position. On one end of the continuum are directors who envision the work of the Israeli counselors in terms of "*symbolic separation*". These directors tend to utilize the Israelis in a functionally separate capacity and see the educational benefits of the Israeli presence as occurring along the representative/symbolic dimension. Near the middle of the continuum are those who want the Israeli staff to integrate into the life of the camp and try to "*balance*" the educational importance of both the representative and personal role of the Israeli in the camp. Finally, at the other end of the continuum are directors who strive for complete *"interpersonal integration"* of the Israeli counselors into the camp. These directors utilize Israeli counselors in a functionally integrated capacity, and conceptualize their educational value in terms of the "little events" of everyday life that occur in the course of interpersonal interaction.

It is worth noting that none of the directors as individuals fall entirely at one end of the spectrum or the other. While some directors stressed integration rather than separation, and vice-versa, in all cases at least some elements of the representative and interpersonal aspects of the Israeli presence was voiced by all directors. The difference between them was in the way each director emphasized one aspect rather than the other. While all the directors whom we interviewed were agreed about the importance of having Israeli staff in their camps, only those who use one of the two "integration" strategies view themselves as responsible for promoting a transformative identity for *both* the Israeli counselor and the American camper and staff.

In summation, when we consider the various ways that directors spoke about their Israeli staff in relation to: the jobs they are assigned; where they eat and sleep; how the Israelis spend their days off; how they as directors involve the Israeli staff in activities falling outside their main job descriptions; what additional roles are played by returning counselors (*vatikim*); how the directors encourage their Israeli staff to bring their "Israeliness" or Israeli identity into their jobs; and finally, how the directors describe the overall role or place of the *shlichim* in the camp – we arrive at the three strategies, "symbolic separation," "balanced integration" and "interpersonal integration.".

These three strategies represent distinct worldviews about the Israel-Diaspora relationship and the role of that relationship in enriching the Jewish lives of campers, counselors, and *shlichim*. Each of the integration strategies pushes forward an alternative model of Israel in camp, in which People-to-People connections anchor the Israel-Diaspora relationships, with a focus on building a richer sense of Jewish belonging for all involved. The symbolic separation strategy maintains the classic Zionist worldview. Israelis who represent Israel in camp are "special" in that they represent Israel. They remain a symbolically distinct group and as a result are not integrated into camp life. The Israelis are there to bring Israel to the camp. Whether or not the *shlichim* benefit in terms of their own Jewish identity is not an explicit consideration. In the "balanced integration" strategy, "Israeli" and "American" Jews remain distinct entities in terms of the organization of camp life and the manner in which the camp encourages interpersonal interactions. However, the Israelis and Americans are equal to one another in that both are Jewish populations contributing to and benefiting from their experience at camp. In the "interpersonal integration" strategy "Israel" and "Diaspora" this pattern is taken one step further. The focus is on individuals, not groups. "Israel" is not an entity that stands apart, but an important resource for the life of the camp implemented in the actions of campers and counselors, each according to their ability (knowledge and experience) and need.

VIGNETTE 3: YACHDAV/SCHOOL-TO-SCHOOL ISRAEL-DIASPORA VIRTUAL MIFGASH

The *Yachdav* School-to-School project is another example of a school-to-school twinning initiative that began as a shared curriculum project and has evolved into something more multi-layered and sophisticated. Like other *mifgashim* programs, highlighted in the vignettes in this section of the book, *Yachdav* is designed to enhance the level of social interaction between Diaspora and Israeli Jews. In this case, the major mode of interaction between the American and Israeli participants is virtual.

Initially, this "virtual *mifgash*" project was built around a series of curricular units that that are designed to enhance and enrich learners exploration of their own Jewish lives and backgrounds by learning about each other. The project includes the exchange of work products between two classrooms, one in Israel and the other in the Diaspora, as well as video-conference meetings. The goals of the project are articulated in their promotional materials as follows:

The Yachdav: School-to-School Israel-Diaspora Virtual Mifgash Program aims to cultivate meaningful connections between Jewish upper elementary grades students in Israel and in the Diaspora. The basis of these connections is in getting both groups in touch, through a mutual learning experience, with what they have in common – Jewish content and values – while at the same time, giving them the opportunity to explore each group's own unique identity as citizens of different cultures and countries (Yachdav Rationale).

The project began in 2004 as an initiative of the Lokey Academy for Jewish Studies at the Leo Baeck Education Center in Haifa. A reorganization in 2009 led to the project coming under the leadership of the Education Department of the Israel Movement for Progressive Judaism (IMPJ). Today, there are 41 schools participating in the project; 20 in the U.S., 21 in Israel, and one in London. The program is offered to any community in the Jewish world.

An initial evaluation study conducted by Grant (2006) explored two questions related to *Yachdav*'s impact and potential: (1) In what way does *Yachdav* enhance the level of social engagement between the students and faculty in the partner schools? And (2) How does *Yachdav* develop attitudes and attachment between Israel and the Diaspora?

Data were gathered from a 90-minute focus group meeting with four educators who teach the *Yachdav* program in Israeli partner schools and an additional one-hour personal interview with another educator. Hour-long face-to-face interviews were conducted with the two curriculum writers and the *Yachdav* program coordinator. In addition, telephone interviews were conducted with four principals and one teacher from four participating schools in Massachusetts and Philadelphia, and three classroom teachers from two different schools in Haifa.

Analysis of these data revealed three central and interrelated issues.

1. Different needs/Shared goals

   While each side of the partnership articulated different needs, they ultimately shared quite similar goals - to foster a deeper understanding and appreciation for the fact that the Jewish world is interconnected and extends far beyond the borders of one's own small community.

2. The impediment of language

   Language barriers between students and faculty create some programming challenges that need to be overcome.

3. Overall fit with curriculum

   The initial *Yachdav* curriculum was designed as a packaged program that did not always fit within the broader educational vision and program schedule of each participating school.

Different needs/Shared goals

Not surprisingly, it appears that the orientation to the project is driven by social, cultural, and organizational factors that are distinct for each side of the partnership. Simply put, the two sides shaped their goals based on their perception of how the *Yachdav* curriculum might be able to meet their needs. For the Israelis, the emphasis was on building a stronger connection to Judaism; for the Americans, the project was about building a stronger connection to Israel and through Israel, the Jewish People.

While each side seems to come from a different starting point, their ultimate goal may be more similar than it first appears. Generally, there was broad consensus among the educators interviewed about the goals within each country. The Israeli teachers all agreed on three primary goals:

1. To develop an understanding that there are Jews outside of Israel and explore what it means to be a Jew outside of Israel;

2. To create a connection to Jewish children outside of Israel; and

3. To begin to understand the idea of *Klal Yisrael.*

For each of the American educators interviewed, the primary goal of the program was to develop a relationship with Israeli peers, where each group would learn what they shared in common with the other. Some hoped this program would dispel what they perceived as an estrangement between the two communities. All hoped that the program would be an engaging way to help their students learn about the history, Land, and People of Israel through this connection.

Based on these statements, developing a strong personal relationship appears to be a stronger goal for the Americans but still central for both sides of the partnership. Both sides want to increase awareness and understanding of the other. Both sides believe that this connection can enhance a feeling of Jewish belonging. Though the angle of orientation for each side is different based on their social and cultural context, at the heart of the matter, the ultimate goal for both sides is to strengthen Jewish identity through a meaningful encounter with other Jews who live elsewhere in the world.

Impediments of language

It appears that the language barriers were greater than anyone initially anticipated. Part of this problem relates to expectations and assumptions that in retrospect may have been better clarified prior to the start of the program. Neither side was particularly satisfied with the exchange of materials. Both expressed frustration that not everything was translated before it arrived. There were also misunderstandings about who would be responsible for translation and where it would take place.

Clearly, the exchange of materials should take place in a language that each side can understand. For an equitable partnership, each side should take responsibility for doing this work. However, teachers at virtually all American congregational schools work just a few hours a week and there are few resources available to translate materials. They also have the advantage of the dominant language. Thus, the Americans typically expect that the translation work will be done on the Israeli side.

It is unlikely that a 13-week curriculum can change such profound cultural expectations on the part of the Americans. In the short-term, this problem can be resolved by clear communication and defining roles in advance of the school year. A longer-term idea may be to build on the "integrate" strategy and work to incorporate the *Yachdav* curriculum into English language classes at the host Israeli school, and Hebrew classes at the host American school. Under this scheme, the students would be more actively engaged in doing their own translations with teacher support and supervision. This would require a much greater commitment to the project in terms of time and integration into the broader vision of the school.

Fit with broader curriculum goals

Perhaps the most important issue relative to the overall success of *Yachdav* is how well the project fits with the broader educational vision and goals of the school. The findings from these interviews yielded impressionistic evidence that raised several questions and concerns.

The *Yachdav* curriculum is perceived as something extra and special at most of the host schools in Israel. For the most part, study of American Jewry or Jews in the world beyond Israel is simply not part of the standard Israeli public school curriculum. Also, the leadership of many Israeli secular schools does not consider the building of Jewish identity to be part of their core educational mission. Further, the educators interviewed in 2006 reported that many of the principals do not fully understand or buy into the goals of the project. Often, the impetus for signing up comes from outside pressure from their American Partnership 2000 community. The Israeli principals see it as a "treat," as a way to free up their own teachers, and maybe as a way to get a free trip to the U.S.

However, in 2009, "Jewish Heritage" became part of the core curriculum in all public schools in Israel. Many schools now augment their heritage curriculum with the *Yachdav* lessons. This seems to work particularly well with schools that have a strong affinity to the project's goals and a well-established relationship with the Leo Baeck Education Center and the IMPJ through a variety of curriculum projects.

On the American side, the *Yachdav* curriculum seems also to be a stand-alone product, though for different reasons. As noted elsewhere in this book, most American religious schools are more likely to connect to Israel in symbolic ways through posters, the Israeli flag, and episodic celebrations around *Tu B'Shvat* and *Yom Ha'atzmaut*, than they are through substantive engagement with Israeli society, history, and culture. Indeed, the *Yachdav* program was attractive to all of the principals interviewed because of the opportunity it offered to deepen the level of engagement beyond what one principal described as "making Israel real instead of just academic."

Each of the principals interviewed saw *Yachdav* both as a way to improve their Israel curriculum in particular and to enhance the level of their school's connection to Israel in general. Yet, none of the schools used *Yachdav* to enrich an already existing program; rather, three of the four principals indicated that they replaced their prior Israel curriculum with *Yachdav*. Thus, it appears that they did not dedicate additional time for Israel study, but rather hoped this more intensive and interactive program would be a more engaging approach than what they had done in the past. Interestingly, one principal began to articulate a vision for how she would build upon the *Yachdav* curriculum across grades, with children and parents, and in formal and informal settings. She said:

I think it could have a tremendous spin off if these relationships do take off – extend it from kids to families. That could really bring people in. The kids who went on the 11/12th grade trip this year, met with Leo Baeck students in Haifa. If these kids remain in the program, we would change our high school program to keep that alive (Grant, 2006, p. 10).

Next Steps

The initial evaluation showed that *Yachdav* enhances the level of social engagement between students and faculty in the partner schools simply because most of these schools had no substantive interaction with the "other" prior to implementing this program. It is also clear that many of the educators on both sides believe that more needs to be done to develop these relationships.

Both American and Israeli educators reported concerns about communication between the partners, translation of materials exchanged between the classes, and expectations about the depth of interpersonal engagement between the students. We also saw that disappointment and frustration with the administrative details, limited logistical support, and technology ran higher among the American schools. Along with this criticism however, we found strong support and commitment to the program on both sides. Most of those interviewed expressed good will in wanting to make it work better for all involved.

The 2006 evaluation study raised several questions that helped direct further planning for *Yachdav*. While shared curriculum is still a component, the overall goal has been re-focused more on building a partnership between schools rather than simply sharing a program. This has resulted in greater customization of materials to better fit with individual schools' schedules, curricular goals, and technology resources. Much more work is being done to link the U.S. and American teachers and not just the students through video-conference calls throughout the year. Recently, the *Yachdav* coordinator began to visit long-term partner schools to conduct on-site professional development with the American teachers. One American long-term partner school has embarked on writing curriculum together with *Yachdav* staff. *Yachdav* staff has also begun arranging home hospitality for American families when they come to visit Israel. For example, one American family joined in the *Pesach* programming of their partner school community when they came to Israel during the holiday break.

As *Yachdav* has evolved, increasing attention is being paid to building long-term relationships between American and Israeli partner school communities of students, parents, and teachers to achieve its ultimate goal of building stronger attachments between Israeli and American Jews. While assessing the success of these endeavors needs further study, there appear to be several key factors that can maximize the potential for a rich partnership and connection to take root. These include: ongoing professional development for teachers on both sides, flexibility in program design to meet individual school's needs, going outside the classroom both virtually through technology and in "real-time" through visits to both partner communities, as well as ongoing evaluation and reflection on practice. As *Yachdav* expands its work, it has the potential to become a framework for sustaining rich connections that endure long beyond the curriculum itself.

NOTES FOR EDUCATORS ON
CONNECTING TO ISRAEL

This section explores a strategy that fosters social contact between Diaspora and Israeli Jews as a central thread for the overall weave of Israel education. Successful person-to-person (P2P) programming is built on social relationships between individuals, which provide participants with direct experience of the Jewish collective. The manner in which these one-to-one connections simultaneously enable personal and Peoplehood experiences is what interests us.

Barry Chazan's (2002b) essay on "The Philosophy of Informal Jewish Education," provides a useful framework for thinking about the connect strategy as a form of informal education. As he writes:

The groups of which we are apart shape our minds, language, and selves in very central ways. Therefore, teaching groups is not simply about transmitting knowledge to all the individuals gathered in one room, but rather is very much about the dynamic role of the collective in expressing and reinforcing values that are part of the culture of the society that created the group (p. 12).

In the vignettes presented in this section, the "dynamic role of the collective" is front and center. Whether in the context of classroom or experiential education, the connect dimension of Israel education is in every aspect about connecting individuals to the collective.

Curricula and pedagogy

Curricula and pedagogy in Israel education generate collective and social Jewish experience in a planned way. Whether through classroom or experiential learning the educational environment itself is thought out in the finest of detail, what Chazan calls a "plan of action."

Curriculum has been generally seen as characteristic of formal rather than informal education and understood in terms of set courses of studies, with lists of subjects to be covered, books to read, ideas to be learned, and tests to be given. However, the more generic concept of curriculum as an overall blueprint or plan of action is very much part of informal Jewish education (p. 9).

For example, when we look at Vignette 2 in this section, on the manner in which summer camp directors integrate Israeli *shlichim* into their camps, we witness a tremendous amount of attention to the mundane aspects of inter-personal interaction. Summer camps that are intentional about connecting Israeli and Diaspora Jews must devote considerable attention in their educational planning to where Israelis and Americans eat, sleep, spend their leisure time, and work together to plan special events. When thought about in this manner, the camp environment becomes an educational platform for Peoplehood, for which the Israeli *shlichim* are an important resource.

The social relationship between Jews is the building block, on top of which a structured educational plan must unfold. Again Chazan's (2002b) notions about informal education support our understanding of how to curricularize the connect strategy:

While it is both flexible and closely related to the lives and significant moments of the learners, this curriculum is rooted in a well-defined body of Jewish experiences and values.... Ultimately the unfolding of the curriculum is determined by the interaction of people with each other and with core experiences. ... The active dialogue back and forth with others is not simply pedagogically useful; it is, in a more basic sense, a pivotal factor in shaping our ideas, beliefs, and behaviors. The principle of interactivity implies a pedagogy of asking questions, stimulating discussions, and engaging the learner. To stimulate interactivity, educators must create an environment which invites learners to listen to each other and to react with dignity and decency (p. 9-10).

For the connect dimension of Israel education to succeed, interpersonal dialogue of the type Chazan describes comes out of the meeting between Israelis and Americans. The "active dialogue back and forth" occurs between the participants and between staff and participants and their communities in a dynamic, yet planful process. The third vignette on the Yachdav school-to-school program points to the importance of two key dimensions:

1. Communication

Clear communication is needed between the partners about expectations and planning, including consideration of the technology and language issues required for establishing on-going and meaningful contact between individuals who live far from one another.

2. Partnership

While each side of the partnership is likely to articulate different needs, they ultimately share quite similar goals - to foster a deeper understanding and appreciation for the fact that the Jewish world is interconnected and extends far beyond the borders of one's own small community. To reach this goal means building a partnership rather than simply sharing a program. The result is customization of materials to better fit each participating institution's schedules, curricular goals, and technology resources in a manner, which includes students, educators, parents, administrators, and members of the board.

Organization

Successful partnership requires overcoming a perception of "us" and "them." The partnership does not sanctify a relationship between "Americans" and "Israelis," but rather generates the experience of membership in a common Jewish People. To accomplish this goal, educational planning and implementation requires a degree of collaboration between the American and Israeli staff that must ensure that participants experience the program as a single Jewish group, rather than two distinct groups spending time together. To break down boundaries and establish "Jewish social relationships" between national groups requires a different organizational logic than most of our institutions currently work by.

From the organizational perspective, the planning of a people-to-people event must focus on the question: How will social contact between Diaspora and Israeli Jews bring concrete educational, institutional, and community building benefits? Instead of focusing narrowly on project planning and implementation, significant staff time must be devoted to establishing partnerships with Israeli institutions, with thought given to how best to integrate staff, parents, administration, and lay leaders into the initiative.

In our experience, many people-to-people programs focus only on the educational benefit for the individual participants, without considering how the people-to-people program also brings benefit to the educational institutions, their staff, and community. People-to-people programs are expensive, involving tremendous financial expense and human resources. Without a clear understanding of the broader benefits, the program is unlikely to sustain itself over the long term at a level of excellent educational quality without framing it as an essential and integral part of a broader communal, educational, and organizational development strategy.

The following two examples show how people-to-people programming can be embedded within a broader strategy, in which the organization and communal benefits of the investment in Israel education are clear.

Chicagoland Jewish High School uses its Israel trip to complement the in-school curriculum with its focus on critical thinking about Jewish life (our integration dimension). As each student is encouraged to develop a sophisticated understanding of Jewish life today, so they are also encouraged to develop informed opinions about complex issues having to do with Israeli society and Israel Diaspora relations (our complicate dimension). The school's affiliation with the Conservative Movement and the Chicago Federation's partnership program with Kiryat Gat serves as the institutional framework for creating a personal sense of connection to Israeli society and for social connections to Israeli

Chicagoland Jewish High School provides an example of an organization that has developed a very sophisticated sense of the benefits for the participant and school community of an Israel trip. The school sponsors a 3-week program during winter vacation organized by USY in Israel. A high percentage of the senior class participates. For example in 2008, a total of 33 out of 39 seniors went on the trip. The school has several goals for the program:

1. Deepen the learning experience at school while in Israel
The goal of the trip is not to produce an exceptional opportunity for religious or spiritual development. Rather, they try and follow the same practices in Israel as they would in the school in Chicago. The rationale behind the trip is that every Jew should have a deep connection to Israel; the trip is not a spark, but a way of deepening connections. The trip just continues practice.

2. Enable critical engagement
The education program focuses on teaching critical thinking and showing participants how to reach sophisticated conclusions through studying contemporary issues. The goal is to grapple with Israel as a complex and intricate society. A significant amount of time is spent looking at grey areas in Israel (security, politics, social problems, poverty, etc.). The educators try to be as dogma-free as possible, allowing participants to come to their own conclusions. "Decisions should be made based on knowledge."

3. Develop partnership program
During the trip, a strong emphasis is placed on meeting Israelis and receiving a variety of perspectives. The trip includes a meeting with students from Kiryat Gat, which is part of the broader development of a partnership with a Kiryat Gat school.

4. Connect to Conservative Movement
Considerable energy is invested to connect students to the Conservative movement in Israel.

5. Impact school culture
The Israel trip's alumni are expected to bring the experience back to the school in order to position Israel as a central part of school culture and raise excitement among younger students about their future trip.

Interview with Rabbi Elliot Goldberg, Director of Religious Life, Chicagoland Jewish High School, quoted in Kopelowitz, Wolf and Markowitz 2009.

Jews. The ultimate measure of success is that the trip to Israel infuses the school culture with excitement about Israel, with younger classes and their parents looking forward to their own future Israel trips. As a result, the trip itself is institutionalized in Chicagoland as an important and central educational platform for Jewish education at the school.

The WCJCC example (next page) shows the reasons why a Jewish community center (JCC) would make such a large investment of its staff resources in partnering programs with JCCs in other countries. The participating JCCs report increased participation of participants and their parents and an overall increase of interest at their Community Centers about issues related to world Jewry. By consciously including three circles of participants at each JCC – teen participants, JCC staff and directors, and Board members and parents - the educational structure of the program is designed to bring about the benefits of increased participation and institution-wide connection to world Jewry.

In summary, the connect dimension begins with social interactions which are carefully planned educational experiences, involving curricula, pedagogical and organizational strategies that enable the social experience to trigger a collective Jewish experience. At its most successful people to people education brings broad educational and organizational benefits to the participating individuals, organizations, and communities.

Based in Jerusalem, The World Confederation of Jewish Community Centers
(WCJCC) is the umbrella organization of more than 1,100 Jewish Community
Centers (JCCs) worldwide. The Tri-Center project partners three JCCs, one in
Israel, one in North America and a third with a JCC in another region of the
world. The vision is that each JCC works to enable a connection between their
local constituents to Jews in other lands and at the same time build the human
resources and organizational support for Jewish Peoplehood related work.

The design of a successful partnership program considers a number of
factors:

1.   Circles of participants
Each project is designèd around three circles. First is the central circle of
participants. A second circle around the core group consists of involved JCC
staff and directors. In the outer circle are Board members of each JCC and
parents who are involved, but in a more selective manner.

2.   Mutuality and inclusion
An essential part of the Partnership process is building trust and confidence
from the primary stakeholders at each JCC and equal levels of participation
from all partners.

3.   Curriculum
Three cross cutting modules that inform all stages of the Partnership
program: 1) building connections, 2) leadership training and 3) volunteer
service.

Research conducted by WCJCC (Kopelowitz, 2010b) on the first Tri-Center
program found that JCC staff attributes increased participation of participants
and their parents at their JCC; and, an overall increase of interest in their
Community Centers about issues related to world Jewry. Program alumni
expressed a strong interest in continued learning about world Jewry, and
have become more active as Jewish leaders since the program.

An earlier version of this case study appears in Kopelowitz and Ravid (2010).

CONCLUDING CASE STUDY – LOOKING AT HOW INTEGRATE, COMPLICATE, AND CONNECT COME TOGETHER AT CAMP HARLAM. CO-AUTHORED WITH VICKI TUCKMAN[23]

Throughout this book, we have been attempting to show how the three core strategies for Israel education of integrate, complicate, and connect can enrich and deepen individual and collective expressions and commitments to Jewish life. The research vignettes are organized around and zoom in on one of the three dimensions to illuminate the specifics of each approach. While we present them as individual strategies, ultimately, these dimensions are closely intertwined and can serve to build upon and reinforce each other in practice.

One way to see how this plays out in the field is through a case study of an educational setting. We have chosen to present a case that depicts a "work in progress" in order to explore the process of moving from vision to reality. This case study is written in collaboration with Rabbi Vicki Tuckman, Director of Jewish Life at Camp Harlam, part of the family of overnight camps within the Union for Reform Judaism (URJ).

For the last several years, the Union for Reform Judaism (URJ) has focused considerable attention on the purposes, nature, and quality of Israel education in its summer camps and Israel programs. In 2008 the URJ received a generous grant from the Legacy Heritage Fund for developing an educational strategy to enhance and strengthen the presence of Israel in the URJ camps and deepen the impact of Israel education on the staff and campers. This work is currently coordinated by Yehudit Werchow, the central Jewish Agency *shlicha* (emissary) for the

---

23 Rabbi Vicki Tuckman is Director of Jewish Life at Camp Harlam. In addition to working for Camp Harlam, Vicki is Rabbi and Director of Education at Temple Micah in Lawrenceville, NJ.

URJ. Werchow's responsibilities include working with the educational leadership of the 13 North American URJ camps and all of the NFTY in Israel programs, through training seminars and consultations.

Werchow sees her mission as helping the camps make Israel a more integral part of daily life. Her work fits closely with the functional integration and interpersonal interaction approaches described in the research presented in Vignette 2 of the "Connect" section. These two approaches are aligned with the notions of Integrate and Connect, two of the three core dimensions of Israel education that we explore throughout this book. In other words, Werchow works with camp leadership to help them articulate their vision of the presence of Israel in their camps and think through what structural and programmatic changes can reshape camp culture so that Israel is more integrated and that Israeli staff are more connected to the rhythms, relationships, and routines of camp life. By integrating and connecting, Israel's presence in camp moves beyond symbolic representation.[24]

Werchow also works to "Complicate Israel" through her work with the summer *shlichim* (Israeli staff), by modeling and engaging them in educational experiences that move away from nostalgic "postcard" representations of Israel into a richer and more nuanced presentation. Essential to these shifts in thinking and doing is the creation of a culture of shared responsibility for "owning" Israel in camp. In other words, the goal is for Israeli staff to become partners with Americans in the process of shaping and creating the presence of Israel in camp. They bring their interests, expertise, and care to program responsibilities and relationships in ways that make Israel more of a shared experience between campers and staff and between American and Israeli staff.

---

24. The introduction to the Connect section of this book discusses the difference between symbolic and other approaches to Israel education.

All of these changes are designed to enhance the potential for
Israel to become part of the entire fabric of Jewish life through
prayer, learning, the physical space of camp, ritual and ceremony,
use of Hebrew language, the arts, sports, and virtually every other
aspect of camp life. As Werchow states,

*We aren't just talking about Israel engagement through some special
programs and activities, but about integrating Israel into our identity. Once
we allow Israel to come in, it becomes part of our Jewish journey. When
Israelis and North Americans learn, experience and educate about Israel
together, it can help both groups to address some of their personal struggles,
generate excitement and inspiration, and build long lasting relationships
amongst them and between them and Israel.*[25]

Ultimately, Werchow's goal is similar to the one we state at the
outset of this book - to see Israel as a resource for Jewish life. She
strives to teach in a way that helps individuals to internalize Israel
into Jewish self-understanding and Jewish collective expression.

This philosophical stance shaped the content of the annual
training seminar for URJ Camp Directors of Education that took
place in Israel in April 2011. The purpose of the seminar was to
explore how Israel education and the Israeli staff who come to
work at URJ camps could be more organically integrated into
camp life. Rather than concentrate exclusively on program
planning however, the seminar was threaded with opportunities
for the participants to explore the question "Why Israel for me?"
This approach was grounded in the assumption that before these
directors could ask their staff and campers to explore the
question of where Israel fits in their lives; they needed to do this
work for themselves.

Integration requires complication and connection

The clearly articulated goal to make Israel a more significant
component of American Jewish identity puts "Integrate" front
and center as the primary focus of Werchow's work. However,

25. Interview with Yehudit Werchow, May 5, 2011

she sees "Complicate" and "Connect" as the means to achieve this greater end. The training seminar in Israel was a time to model some of the rich possibilities for achieving these three ends.

Tefilah is one example of how all three dimensions came into play during the seminar. For example, the Shabbat morning service was created in partnership with Esteban Gottfried and his musicians from *Beit Tefila Israeli*. The service was created to model an experience that was both true to the spirit of Reform prayer and that would be welcoming and engaging for Israelis who were likely to be unfamiliar with innovative prayer and with Reform Judaism. Another goal for this prayer experience was to model ways that Israel can be richly integrated into worship. As Werchow said:

We wanted to create islands of comfort for the Israelis by using familiar Hebrew poetry and music in a way that would reflect the themes of the tefilah, and to introduce the North American staff to ways to integrate Israeli modern culture and Israel in general to new areas of their Jewish experience.

The prayer service also reinforced the idea that the Israeli staff don't "own" all things Israel at camp by having an American staff person recite the prayer for the State of Israel. Though this is a small act, it has high symbolic value.

This experience integrated Israel into a regular Jewish practice (*tefilah*), it complicated the prayer through the use of Israeli melodies and supplemental readings, and it connected Israelis and Americans through the shared experience where there was something familiar and strange for both. Thus, Israel became a part of a shared *Jewish* experience that was designed to foster a deeper appreciation for how Israeli culture can enrich American Reform *tefilah*, while also strengthening *Jewish* identity. The end goal was to inspire and reinforce feelings of collective belonging, demonstrating how worship becomes a richer experience of Jewish Peoplehood through this cross-cultural shaping of the experience.

Another example of integrating Israel into a Jewish experience was a workshop with the Israeli poet Roni Somek. Though few of the educators are fluent, Somek conducted the workshop in Hebrew. He taught several of his poems that playfully describe the tension and synergy between Biblical Hebrew, modern Hebrew, and everyday life in Israel. In their evaluation forms many of the participants indicated that the workshop was an eye-opening experience and that it demonstrated that learning Hebrew was a strong vehicle for Jewish identity building and could surely serve the same function for their campers as well.

Camp Harlam - Case Study

The impact of these efforts is ultimately to help camp educational leadership think in new and different ways about Israel education. Many Jewish overnight camps in America have come to recognize that a more thoughtful, deeper, integrated Israel program is necessary in order to bring a rich and modern Israel to their camp communities.

The following "case study" will be examining the changes taking place in one particular camp in the URJ system, Camp Harlam. The case is based on a combination of analysis of written documents including vision statements, curricular materials, planning documents, on-site visits, and a series of conversations between Grant, Werchow, and Tuckman. This process of investigation and analysis has allowed Tuckman to engage in serious reflection on her practice. As Sinclair (2011) notes, this form of practitioner inquiry is a process of "looking back at the educational act, using as much documentation as appropriate or necessary" (p. 923) in order to deepen the practitioner's knowledge of her educational practice and to contribute to pedagogical content knowledge (Shulman, 1987) of the particular subject - in this case Israel education. In other words, this form of practitioner inquiry serves dual purposes. It enriches a portrait of Israel Education at Camp Harlam and it engages the practitioner in a dialogical and reflective process that raises significant issues about the challenges and opportunities in developing a new way of thinking about, and subsequently doing, Israel education in "real time" at camp.

Several significant changes took place at Harlam in the last few years philosophically, structurally, and programmatically with regard to Israel and the relationships between the Israeli and American staff. These changes, which will be described below, fit squarely within both the "integrate" and "connect" dimensions for Israel engagement. One of the main insights drawn from the experiences of these past few years for Camp Harlam has been that the educators/teachers need to be constantly thinking about ways to integrate Israel. There are numerous moments that have the potential to be infused with Israel, but without thought or planning, the educational moment passes.

Camp Harlam has a made a long-term investment of time, money, and training into having a sizable cohort of Israeli staff, who serve as a major educational pillar of camp life. Yet, even with the current level of educational commitment and planning, much of the "connecting" between the Israelis and Americans is still left to friendships that form in an organic and serendipitous manner from the experience of overnight camp. Camp Harlam leadership is now thinking about how to be more proactive and focused in fostering more meaningful and personal dialogue, helping both Israelis and Americans to learn from each other and grow together. This is grounded in the belief that it is vital for each to see "the other" as a way to strengthen Jewish identity and commitment to Judaism.

At Camp Harlam, the complicate dimension of Israel education remains a challenge. Indeed, we feel that in general, this dimension is perhaps the most difficult one to achieve. As we will see, steps are also being taken to "complicate" Israel at Camp Harlam through the *shiur* (formal education) sessions and other programming; but, this endeavor is fraught with challenges relating to prior assumptions, expectations, and expertise of both the American and Israel staff. Perhaps, it is this final frontier of complicating Israel that will take it out of the symbolic and representational realm and ultimately lead to deeper integration into Jewish life and stronger Peoplehood connections.

The Chazon Training - Clarifying and Articulating Purposes

The process of seriously reflecting on the overarching purposes for Israel education and awareness began in 2009 when a member of the professional staff, Rabbi Vicki Tuckman, participated in a multi-year training program, called CHAZON. The program, funded and implemented by the Avi Chai Foundation, is designed to help camps thoroughly analyze every aspect and component of their Israel education and programming. Yet before having participants dive into the "nuts and bolts" of programming, the main thrust of the four training sessions was to ask the macro questions:

- For what purpose does any camp engage in Israel education?

- What is "the Israel" your particular camp wishes to teach? How is camp consistent with that message and engaged in creating dynamic curriculum and meaningful programming to weave Israel into Jewish programming and various camp activities and moments?

- Who are the stakeholders and key players at your camp who will help realize this vision?

- How do we create better partnerships between American and Israeli staff?

- How do we formally establish a cadre of people who see themselves as "Israel educators?"

This process lead the Harlam team to create a document called an "Israel Ideological Framework", along with a plan to educate staff and the clergy and educators who serve as faculty,[26] to

---

26 Typically, faculty for URJ camps comes from rabbis, cantors, and educators from the region who come to camp for two-week sessions. Thus, the faculty rotates throughout the summer.

understand Camp Harlam's vision for Israel education and to create programming and conversations along these foundational ideas. This was a radical change at Camp Harlam. While Israel was identified as a vitally important component of camp, the purposes and goals for Israel education had never been defined by the professional leadership nor put into a written form. Thus, the current *mishlachat* or American staff determined any Israel lessons or programming. While these moments may have been filled with *ruach* (spirit), they lacked sophistication or educational depth. Furthermore, the programming was repetitive as well as inconsistent as the camp was not instituting a "spiral curriculum" to grow with the campers as they rose up through the ranks of camp. Lastly, they failed to present any sense of contemporary issues and realities in Israel. Campers were more often taught to milk cows, dress up like IDF soldiers, and Israeli dance; rather than creating a foundational knowledge for understanding the depth and personality of a modern Israel. There was no attempt to engage the campers in lessons about a "real" Israel filled with thousands of years of rich and deep history. Rather, the focus was on the mythic Israel. Like teaching that George Washington chopped down a cherry tree as a part of American history, the Harlam educational team ignored the complexities that ultimately turn out to be more compelling in the end.

The Ideological Framework was built around four key points that answer the key question "Why are we engaged in Israel education at Camp Harlam?"

- Israel is a tool for, and essential facet of, building Jewish Identity.

- *Ahavat Yisrael* is an important Jewish value we wish to teach our camp community.

- It is our desire for our community to feeling connected to the Land, People, and State of Israel.

- Our commitment to the *mishlachat* program.

- We strongly encourage travel to Israel.

These points consider the important role that Israel can play in both individual Jewish identity formation and in cultivating a stronger sense of belonging to *Am Yisrael*, the Jewish People. They also stress the need to foster an active relationship with Israel through travel and by cultivating mutual love between Diaspora and Israeli Jews.

Step 1: Structural and Programmatic Integration

The first steps towards increased integration were actually a series of sophisticated moves that entailed a number of staff and departmental reorganizations. Until the summer of 2011, the Israeli staff worked under the supervision of the *Rosh Mishlachat* (the head of the delegation) and functioned as its own division as it does at many camps. Though Israeli staff at these camps almost always lives in bunks with campers, they tend to work as specialists (i.e., waterfront, sports, camping, and nature), not as counselors. The result at Harlam is that the Israeli staff was not fully integrated into the educational vision of the camp. Their engagement in "educational" programming was limited to planning and implementing "*Yom Yisrael.*" Planning for this big event usually takes place at night or during "off periods" which creates a separation between the American staff, and from the daily educational activities. In a way, quite similar to what we described in Vignette 2 of the Connect section, this perpetuates a distancing and reinforces a symbolic role for the Israel staff as representatives of Israel rather than simply Israelis who are an organic part of the Jewish experience of camp.

In 2009, Anat Katzir, who had previously served as the *Rosh Mishlachat* and a member of the athletic staff at Harlam, became the Assistant Director of Jewish Life, as well as continuing her role as *Rosh Mishlachat*. In this new position she began reporting to Rabbi Tuckman, the Assistant Director/Director of Jewish Life. This shift in role paved the way for a more active and deliberate attempt to integrate Israel into many more varied

Lisa Grant and Ezra Kopelowitz, with Vicki Tuckman

aspects of camp life including the formal *shiur* process, special
Israel Projects, bringing the presence and *ruach* of the *mishlachat*
into the *Chadar Ochel* (dining hall), and weaving Israel education
into the daily schedule and unit programs. As an Israeli with a
strong Jewish identity and a well-formed attachment to Reform
Judaism, it was natural for Anat to weave Israel and "Jewish
education" together because this is the "normative" way in which
she views herself as a Jew and as a professional educator. This
change was intended to make Israel both a special focus and a
part of the regularities of camp life. As Anat said:

*Israel is part of the continuum; it's not a separate entity, but integral to all of
camp. We no longer see the Israeli staff as emissaries, but as partners. We
are doing more to engage the American staff in the Israel conversation (and
programming) than ever before. We are doing more to break the barriers
between the two groups.*

The barriers to which Katzir refers are breaking down in several
ways. In 2010, Tuckman and her staff totally revamped the camp
curriculum. Previously, the curriculum was built around an annual
rotating theme of God, *Torah*, and Israel. In other words, Israel
would be on the educational docket once every three years.
Tuckman realized that this approach perpetuated the isolation
and separation of Israel from other aspects of Jewish life. The
new spiral curriculum rests upon the themes of "*tikkun olam*"
(repairing the world) and "*tikkun middot*" (character development
via Jewish texts and Judaic values). The exciting part of the new
curriculum is that it allows Israel to be woven into an assortment
of topics. Israel, therefore, can become an integral part of the
conversation without necessarily becoming the focal point. For
example, an activity based on learning names and building
community might start with a text study of Zelda's poem
"Everybody Has a Name" (Zelda, 2004) with an explanation of
Zelda's role as a modern Israeli poet. A nature hike in the woods
might integrate conversations about the Israelites wandering in
the wilderness, connecting one of the summer's *Torah* portions
into a weekday activity. An activity in the "*Teva* Garden" could be

making Israeli salad and a discussion of vegetables currently grown on Israeli kibbutzim.

In 2011, Tuckman assumed official supervision of the *mishlachat*. This was done specifically to increase communication and collaboration between Israeli staff and the Camp's Department of Jewish Life. Before 2011, the *mishlachat* met on a weekly basis more as a friendship/support group, without a hands-on liaison from the professional staff. These meetings focused either on acclimating to the camp environment or working on Israel Day. Moving the *mishlachat* to the Department of Jewish Life was intended to add more substance and long-range vision to the Israel programming. It was clear that someone on a higher level needed to weave together the disparate activities not just throughout the summer, but also from summer-to-summer. Perhaps most important, it was imperative for the *Rosh Mishlachat* to see him/herself as a "Jewish educator." This was a subtle yet profound shift in focus, not just for the *Rosh Mishlachat* but also for the camp community, as it was asking people to integrate Israel and Jewish education into one seamless rubric.

In 2011, Tuckman also took a very active role in the *Yom Yisrael* planning which brought it more into the camp's overall vision for Israel Education, rather than solely the *mishlachat's* vision for what Israel education should be. The intent was to create a *Yom Yisrael* that would not be a superficial taste of Israel, but rather a celebration/culmination of a series of experiences throughout the summer that were developmentally appropriate for different age groups and linked more closely to the Israel themes for each of the camp units.

The first step in this process was changing the planning team so that there would be shared responsibility for the program between Israeli staff and Americans. The American staff charged with this task came from among the Cornerstone Fellows, a program sponsored by the Foundation for Jewish Camp, in which counselors returning for a third year participate in special intensive training prior to the summer season. These young adults are clearly committed to Jewish camp and the goal is to support and develop them even further so they begin to see themselves as Jewish educators.

Additional steps towards greater integration took place both structurally and programmatically. Educational programming was redesigned to make Israel more integral to more aspects of every day in camp. In addition to the *mishlachat*, several other camp functions were absorbed into the Department of Jewish life in 2011 including a *teva* (nature) program, hiking, and *Tzofim*, the Israeli scouts. These changes were designed to support the staff in becoming more intentional as Jewish educators and not just activities specialists. Their "professional" identity from the start of camp was to see themselves as members of the "Jewish Life" Department.

The changes in *Tzofim* are a good illustration of the integration of more Israel educational content in these new areas of the Department of Jewish Life. Each summer, two Israeli teens and a supervisor come to Camp Harlam as representatives of *Tzofim*, the Israeli scouts. Their job is to bring Israel to camp using the informal education methods of the scouting movement to which they belong. Until the reorganization in 2011 the scouts were considered a part of the Adventure Department. This meant that the flavor and focus of the *Tzofim* program was on the outdoor and challenge elements. The fact that the staff were from Israel, and that some of the "outer" features of the campsite were Israel-themed or in Hebrew, was incidental. It does not mean that Israel education was not happening at *Tzofim*, but that was not its primary purpose. In 2011, the *Tzofim* were named as "Jewish Life Specialists" and developing Jewish identity and an awareness/love of Israel became explicit goals for their work.

Another desired change was the simple task of making Jewish/Israel learning fun and hands-on. *Tzofim* has always been a beloved activity and place at Camp Harlam. By placing the *Tzofim* rotation under the rubric of Jewish learning, and naming it as a *"shiur"* period, it re-branded the very meaning of Jewish learning.

Shiur often has the reputation at camp for sitting in a circle discussing a Jewish topic; games and activities are often used to enhance the 50-minute period, but it is hard to shake its bad reputation as being slightly better than religious school. "*Shiur*" transformed into true "experiential" learning by spending a period at *Tzofim* (other rotations included hiking, gardening, and faculty-led activities).

These changes were in keeping with Tuckman's long-term goal to create compelling experiences that will lead to instilling strong Jewish values. To achieve this goal, Tuckman designed a spiral curriculum that follows a developmentally appropriate learning sequence. Each unit has a specific educational theme with the Israel component linked to that specific unit. For example, Carmel's (entering 3rd and 4th grade) Israel theme is geography/places in *Eretz Yisrael. Arava* (entering 7th grade) is the exploration of popular Israeli culture. The main thrust of these themes is to provide new Israel programming for the campers each summer, especially for those campers who begin camp as eight year olds and continue through their "Israel summer" at the end of 10th grade. The Israel themes become more complex with age, while remaining cognizant that not all campers have been attending camp since the beginning of the curriculum. It is the job of the educational leadership and camp clergy (faculty members) to gauge the campers' educational knowledge and fill in gaps as needed. The plan is to "complicate" Israel as the campers get older (towards high school) in order to prepare them for a high school NFTY trip or when they travel to Israel in college.

Step 2: Building Connections

The structural and educational changes in the Department of Jewish Life naturally increase the quality and quantity of interaction between Israeli and American staff in camp. As noted, it is very important to Camp Harlam to have a sizable *mishlachat*. The goal is to have an Israeli counselor living in every bunk in order to maximize the opportunity for personal relationships to

Lisa Grant and Ezra Kopelowitz, with Vicki Tuckman

develop between campers and counselors, as well as the inter-personal relationships amongst staff.

American and Israeli staff members do encounter cultural hurdles, which frequently need to be worked through, but this does not detract from the ideology that Israel "becomes real" through dialogue and the development of authentic relationships. The reality of the geographic, cultural, and linguistic distance between Americans and Israelis can be softened when the "distance" can, literally, be erased. The Israel that Camp Harlam leadership wants their campers to know is not the Israel of CNN or from a textbook, but the Israel organically brought to them by Yael, their bunk counselor, or Ori, their soccer specialist. Israel becomes much more real in the quiet moments: learning a new Hebrew phrase, looking at a someone's family picture by the Dead Sea, hearing Israeli rap music during "clean up" time, a simple conversation about life on a kibbutz or how it feels to serve in the army. So often the power of relationships come from seeing the commonalities, which happens simply from getting to know another and being together.

There are several other opportunities for staff to connect at a richer level. Supported by outside organizations such as the Avi Chai Foundation and the Foundation for Jewish Camp (FJC), camp leadership is continually on the lookout for American counselors who have been to Israel and are returning to camp for a second or third year. These staff are then encouraged to work more closely with Israeli staff both to strengthen their social connections and to help them internalize more of a sense of responsibility to Israel in their work.

One area of great potential for strengthening and modeling meaningful connections is between the camp's Cornerstone Fellows and the *mishlachat*. As noted, the Cornerstone Fellows are third year staff members who participate in a special leadership development program. Many of these fellows have participated in other camp leadership programs, such as the *Olim* Program. They tend to be highly motivated staff members, who want to be change agents at camp. They appear committed to bringing greater substance to Israel education at camp and this is a significant part of their program portfolio.

Despite their motivation, the fellows noted that there were a number of logistical and conceptual challenges in working with *mishlachat* staff on Israel education in general and in the planning of *Yom Yisrael* in particular. Several of the fellows expressed frustration and disappointment that they were not more active partners in the process. In essence, they felt they did not have equal voices in the program design and thus felt no sense of ownership.

The fellows offered a number of constructive recommendations for how to build stronger connections between Israeli and American staff at camp. They stressed the need for camp leadership to send out strong messages, starting during staff week and continuing throughout the summer, that Israel education is important to everyone at camp. They also suggested that more opportunities are needed for Americans and Israeli staff to connect to each other by partnering in all program development, not just Israel-related programs. They felt that Israeli culture could have a more organic presence in camp through more informal conversations and experiences during free time, rather than only "meeting" Israel through formal encounters and programs. Speaking to *Yom Yisrael* in particular, they suggested that the American staff needed to become greater stakeholders in the program and not cede the time to the Israelis.

Step 3:   Complicating: The Next Frontier

An impressive amount of work has taken place at Camp Harlam in the last few years to better integrate Israel into everyday life at camp and to increase the formal and informal connections between American and Israel staff. It seems that important groundwork has been laid to enable further progress in making Israel a vital resource for Jewish life at camp and hopefully, beyond. At this stage, however, there is still a sizable gap between vision and reality. One of the keys to narrowing that gap appears to rest with the "complicating" factor. On one hand, the educational leadership is on board with the idea that greater depth, detail, nuance, and complexity need to be introduced to create a more compelling weave of Israel experiences in camp. On the other hand, there are many obstacles yet to overcome in achieving a more multi-layered and textured approach to Israel education in camp.

One of the core challenges of complicating relates to the reality of working with two groups of staff who may not be fully committed or fully prepared to teach in this more complicated approach. The first group is made up of young adults with little to no professional background as educators. The second is a rotating cadre of education faculty consisting of rabbis, cantors, and educators from the camp's region who come to camp for two-week sessions. The former group does not yet see themselves as educators, and the latter, while professionals, are for the most part not well grounded in Israel education or in informal educational methods that fit better in the camp environment than standard classroom teaching.

Changing expectations about roles and responsibilities

As noted, one of the greatest challenges to making Israel a more integral and connected part of Jewish life at camp has to do with the question of ownership. There are several factors mitigating the Camp Harlam leadership's goal for developing a stronger partnership and a sense of mutual responsibility for Israel education. Many of the Israeli staff come to camp understanding that it is their job to represent Israel as enthusiastically and positively as they can. This means they may resist initiatives that seek to explore some of the more difficult and contentious areas of contemporary Israel. For instance, during a 2011 site visit to camp, an American faculty member described how he was discouraged by an Israeli staff member from showing a segment of a film about the Women of the Wall.[27]   The film documents the organization's growth and legal battles to obtain the right to for women to pray in a *tallit* and read from the *Torah* at the Western Wall in Jerusalem. It includes scenes of verbal abuse and arrests of women attempting to exercise this right. The Israeli was concerned that seeing Jewish police arresting Jewish women would make the campers uncomfortable and confused.

Most of the Israeli staff members come to camp with minimal to no exposure to liberal American Judaism and minimal to no sense of themselves as Jewish educators. There are also staff members who consider themselves more "Israeli" or "secular" than Jewish. Placing them in an intentionally Jewish environment can be alienating and most do not have the words (at least at the beginning of the summer) to explain the internal conflict they experience. Some of the Israeli staff has never heard of Reform Judaism before applying to work at an American overnight camp. Thus their first significant exposure to liberal Judaism occurs at the training seminar in Israel just six weeks prior to their arrival in America. They arrive at camp and are immediately taken to rural Pennsylvania, where they encounter 200 plus staff members, and the often jarring experiences of progressive Jewish practices such as egalitarian prayer, women rabbis, and the reciting of the Mourner's *Kaddish* at every service.

They need to quickly acclimate to American Judaism, while serving as quasi teachers and feeling the pressure of being "representatives" of Israel. These limiting factors tend to reinforce a sense of distance from the mainstream of camp life

---

27 Women of the Wall is an international and interdenominational group of women who come together to pray at the Western Wall in Jerusalem on the morning of each new month. Their website states their mission is "to achieve the social and legal recognition of our right, as women, to wear prayer shawls, pray and read from the Torah collectively and out loud at the Western Wall." The group has encountered numerous and regular obstacles in achieving their mission, ranging from verbal and physical harassment to arrests for wearing a tallit and/or carrying a Torah scroll. For more information see: http://womenofthewall.org.il/

for many of these staff members, which add to the challenge of integrating Israel into the overall Jewish experience of camp.

Again, *Tzofim* provides a good illustration of how this plays out in daily life at camp. In 2011, the scouts created a "mini-Israel" that included a bunk decorated with a variety of Hebrew bumper stickers, Israeli flags strung up between trees, a giant map/game of Israel, and the "Israel trail," a guided walk with stations along the way that take the campers from the Carmel Forest to Tel Aviv, to the Dead Sea and Eilat. All campers in the Junior Camp unit (3rd – 7th grade) spent at least one and sometimes two sessions with the *Tzofim* as part of their "*shiur*" rotations.

Watching the scouts at work during a site visit to camp, it was clear that they were energetic and enthusiastic and the campers appeared to enjoy their time with them. We observed a session with campers who had just completed the Israel trail walk.

From what we saw, it appears that the Israel content to the *Tzofim* experience remained largely in the mythic realm with only very superficial integration with Jewish life. For example, at the end of their "hike," the scouts gathered the campers in a circle and did a short debrief of the experience. They gave out prizes for campers who came wearing something with Hebrew letters. One of the prizes was a pen that had a tiny scroll with *tefillat ha'derech* (the traveler's prayer) in it. The scouts glossed right over that (perhaps not knowing themselves what it was), but Tuckman interrupted and asked the campers if they knew what the prayer was for. She then gave a brief explanation of how and when this prayer is recited, seeing this as a teachable moment to create a stronger bridge between Israel and Jewish identity development.

While the primary goal of the scouts is to bring Israel to camp, Tuckman clearly would like them to see their job as connected to the overall Enduring Understandings of *tikun olam* and *tikun midot*. Making these connections more substantive and explicit will require significantly more work with these young staff members to help them think about how they can bring both more Israel and more Jewish content to their activities. Indeed, this may be a place where a more mature and seasoned American Jewish educator could partner effectively with the *Tzofim* both in program planning and mentoring. This type of active partnership would also do more to integrate Israel into the broader education program. It would connect Israeli staff more closely with an American partner and it would result in more complicated and textured experiences of Israel and not simply a fun walk in the woods on a simulated Israel trail.

The obstacles to complicating do not rest only with the Israeli staff, however. As noted, the Cornerstone Fellows are among the American staff members with the greatest amount of experience in Israel. In conversation they expressed a desire to engage in Israel programming, but did not yet accept that they have Israel expertise. This was apparent when they spoke about how Israeli and American staff might work together to build a stronger partnership, saying that the American staff could bring their programming expertise and the Israeli staff their Israel knowledge. This remark suggests that they do not yet see the value of how their Israel stories, as American Jews, could contribute to Israel education and a strengthening of Jewish Peoplehood at camp.

Part-time staff, full-time expectations

The temporal nature of camp staff presents significant obstacles to cultivating a high quality educational team. First, there is almost complete turnover of the *mishlachat* every year. There is also tremendous turnover among the young adult American staff. A related problem, but one that has a separate set of challenges as well, is the education faculty, rabbis, cantors, and educators who have full-time jobs elsewhere and come to camp for short sessions. Thus, they are likely to see their stint at camp as peripheral to their core responsibilities. They are often not well versed in methods of informal education and may be reluctant to engage in significant conversations or learning about how to translate the camp's vision for Israel education into practice in their own teaching.

162 | P a g e

The contrast is notable when comparing the lessons of different teachers in camp. As noted earlier, Anat Katzir, a long-time Harlam staff member who served as the *Rosh Mishlachat* for many years, is currently an Assistant Director of Jewish Life. Among her responsibilities at camp is teaching in the *Arava* Unit (entering 7th grade). The Summer 2011 Israel theme for this unit was "Personalities and Historical Figures in Israeli Culture." Her ability to complicate Israel for her campers is seen in contrast to a lesson given by two of the visiting faculty. Katzir described how her goal for this unit was to teach about some of the tensions between the Orthodox establishment and secular society in Israeli culture and to show how many secular Israelis are seeking and experimenting with religious expression outside of Orthodoxy. She strove to teach that these secular Israelis are not Reform Jews in the same way as her American campers, but that they are struggling to find their relationship with Jewish tradition. Her lessons were built around the music of several contemporary artists who are pushing the boundaries and exploring what it means to be a Jew in secular Israeli society today.

In comparison with this nuanced and textured approach to a complicated issue is another class in the *Arava* unit on Jewish heroes that was taught by two rabbis who were among the visiting faculty at camp in the summer of 2011. The campers were divided into small groups and given a short summary of the lives of various important figures in Jewish history from David Ben Gurion to Sandy Koufax, from Henrietta Szold to Molly Picon. Each group gave a very brief report on their hero and then they voted for their top three choices to induct into the "Jewish Hall of Fame." Aside from introducing campers to an array of notable Jews, the lesson did not seem to explore any kind of big idea or key question, such as Katzir's goal of exploring secular Israelis' development of their own form of Jewish expression.

Tuckman has dedicated a lot of thought to creating conceptual and organizational structures that will enable the integration of Israel into the cultural and social fabric of camp in a more organic way. While the frameworks are in place, the reality in the classroom is inconsistent at best. For example, the Israel theme in 2011 for *K'far Noar*, campers entering 9th grade, was "Politics and Government" with the goal of introducing the concept of *Medinat Yisrael* (the State of Israel) as distinct from *Eretz Yisrael* (the Land of Israel). This seems to be a sophisticated topic rich in potential for exploring complex issues. Some of the specific topics of the *Limud* sessions included: Current Events (as reported by a young staff member just back from Israel); Reform Judaism in Israel (with a focus on Women of the Wall); Exploring How do I feel about Israel; and, an experience with the *Tzofim*. The contrast between two lessons we observed in 2011 shows some of the challenges of working with a visiting faculty who may not be prepared to teach at the desired level of sophistication and complexity that these education goals warrant.

The first was billed as a class to explore personal relationships and connections to Israel. However, rather than inviting the campers to share their questions or experiences and facilitating a discussion, the teacher proceeded to lecture for over 15 minutes on the history of Israel while the campers were sitting in the sun. Neither the setting nor the methods of instruction were particularly conducive to learning in this informal setting.

Another lesson provided a more hopeful example. This was a session taught by a rabbi on Zionism. He gave the campers a handout that included brief descriptions of different ideological strains of Zionism - political, cultural, religious, etc. He then posed several rich questions and led the group in a discussion that offered the opportunity for critical thinking and reflection such as:

- Is there a unique Jewish culture that all Jews share? If not, what unites us?

- Is it essential to preserve the Jewish character of the state even at the expense of non-Jewish citizens?

- Do we still need Zionism today?

While the conversation that ensued was more teacher than camper-driven, this lesson introduced these learners to several compelling questions that get at the heart of complicated contemporary conversations about Judaism, the Jewish State, and the Jewish People.

Bringing it all together

As this case suggests, careful deliberation about the purposes and the crafting of a well-aligned spiral curriculum for Israel education is essential to building a strong foundation for integrating and connecting Israel more closely with the overarching Jewish educational goals and processes of camp. However, as Tuckman acknowledges, the work to date has only scratched the surface of what might be done. There is still a significant gap between vision and reality, both in terms of the quality and frequency of active partnering between Israel and American staff in program development and teaching, and in terms of the depth and sophistication of Israel-related content in these programs. Complicating Israel requires educators who are committed to this approach, reflective about their practice, and willing to move away from mythic and superficial representations and explore the more serious questions and challenges that are core to understanding the multiple dimensions of Israel and its relationship to Jewish life.

Given the challenges of high turnover, part-time and under-trained staff as noted above, the work of embedding the ideas, values, and commitment to richer and more complicated integration of Israel into the educational programs at camp and fostering deeper connections between Americans' and Israelis' needs must begin with and be modeled by key staff members of the Department of Jewish Life with greater seniority and longevity in camp - the *Rosh Mishlachat* and the Assistant Directors of Jewish Life. The Cornerstone Fellows are another group of staff that appear ready and willing to engage in deeper reflection about and participation in Israel education. Working with this limited number of staff throughout the year and in an intensive way during training week can help to sophisticate their practice. Thus, they will come to camp ready to mentor and partner with other Israeli and American staff. These two steps may help the seeds that were planted at Harlam over the past few summers to take root and grow into richer and multi-dimensional Israel engagement.

CONCLUSION

As we note at the outset of the book, Israel education is a persistent dilemma in Jewish education with a long-term pattern of practices that fail to inspire and engage or to make the case that Israel is integral to contemporary American Jewish life. This book builds on a growing body of scholarship and our own research experience to offer new ways of thinking about and doing Israel education. We believe that success depends on a shift away from an educational paradigm that focuses exclusively on Israel as a means for reinforcing Diaspora Jewish identity through an expression of solidarity and support for Israel to one that sees Israel as a resource for the multiple dimensions of individual and collective Jewish life wherever it is lived.

This book offers a conceptual roadmap for the new paradigm:

Israel education should be grounded in the idea that engagement with the multiple dimensions of the Land, People, and State of Israel is an essential part of Jewish education and is integral to cultivating a rich sense of mutuality and meaning. Successful Israel education, like a successful Jewish education, enables one to live a rich and meaningful life.

This mutuality and meaning paradigm is framed around three principles that we outlined in the Introduction and brought to life through the research vignettes throughout the book. We reiterate them here as a way to recap and highlight our key points and offer some key take-away ideas for those who wish to join us in promoting this paradigm.

Integrate, complicate and connect are codes which refer to three interrelated educational strategies, each with a clear set of theories and practices that we have sketched in the vignettes and notes for educators in this book.

The three principles of the mutuality and meaning paradigm

1. Integrate

Israel is integral to Judaism and the collective Jewish experience wherever it is lived; as such, at its best, Israel education is integrated into the life of Jewish educational institutions, including the training and support of faculty and staff, the manner in which they work as a team, and the pedagogy and curricular dimensions of Jewish education.

We integrate by bringing multiple representations of Israel into all aspects of Jewish living, with the goal of making Israel a more active and integral part of the Jewish educational landscape. All of this must take place with acute awareness of the opportunities for and impediments to creating a culture that supports deeper integration and engagement at multiple levels.

Integration depends on creating a culture that connects people – collaboration is at the core. Israel education succeeds when it generates meaningful interactions with others, including students, educators, administrators, and lay leaders, ideally interacting with one another. The result is to move beyond episodic and ceremonial experiences of Israel in which participants deepen and expand knowledge and are motivated to apply that knowledge in situations that that are compelling and engaging. Success is measured by participants' perceptions of Israel as relevant to Jewish life as lived and their increased motivation to engage with Israel, along with other areas of their Jewish lives.

Key elements that we can distill from the research suggest the following steps need to occur for Israel to become a more integral and integrated part of the Jewish educational enterprise:

✓ Leadership of the educational institution must clearly articulate the purpose of Israel education and convey how it fits into a vision and goals for Jewish education.

✓ This process is best carried out with the "committed core" of stake-holders who already actively express Israel commitments and behaviors. These stakeholders should be diverse, coming from key populations and organizational areas. The goal is to bring them into collaboration with one another.

✓ Begin by activating the committed core to work on an area that has strategic value to the success of the institution – measured in amount of participation, number of members or constituents, and budgets. If the goal is to make Israel education relevant to each individual, then it must also be relevant to the future prosperity of the institution.

✓ Pay attention to connecting elements within the life of the institution, the points in time and space that enable members to feel part of the Jewish People. Build on the Israel dimension at these key points, to inject enthusiasm, excitement and intellectual stimulation into a lived Jewish life.

✓ Nurture the committed core and widen the circle. Provide key stakeholders with the resources they need to create opportunities for discussion, planning, and participation. They will choose what is interesting and relevant to their lives, you help them figure out the possibilities and connect to the institution's long term interests. Ask them to invite their friends and colleagues to join.

2. Complicate

Israel is a multi-vocal, multi-layered, textured weave that affords the possibility for intellectual, emotional, spiritual, and social engagement with the Land, People, and State of Israel in a way that cultivates a rich sense of belonging and commitment to the Jewish collective. Success is measured by Israel becoming part of an individual's lived life, and as such, Israel becomes complicated. Discord, argument, and debate are critical; otherwise, Israel remains superficial and relatively inconsequential. Board members will argue with one another and their organizations' professionals about vital issues. Family members, who love one another dearly, will often fight over issues they hold dear. The same should be true for Israel and all other matters integral to Jewish life.

Our research suggests that four steps are essential for complicating Israel in a rich and formative way:

- ✓ Think big. What are the big contributions that Israel education can make to your organization or program? Big ideas of necessity call for supple and complex thinking. If Israel education is driven by those big ideas then complexity and mature thought is sure to follow.

- ✓ Begin by recasting myths – look at the stories that people find meaningful and the ceremonies and events that make Israel and the Jewish People come alive in the annual calendar. Promote discussion about their relevance to individuals' lives today. Shift the symbols of what could be described as a "dead past" into a usable present.

- ✓ Examine the content of what is being taught, being mindful of the need to reframe old myths into more sophisticated and compelling narratives that present the many layers of both the ideal and the real Israel and also allow learners to grapple with the tension between them. If no one dissents, if everyone applauds, if no one asks a critical question, you probably have not succeeded.

- ✓ Deepen educators' knowledge through serious, substantive, and ongoing professional learning about Israel. This includes, but it is certainly not limited to, ensuring that all who teach Israel participate in Israel trips geared specifically for educators. The learning must continue back in the home institution through formal study about Israeli history and society, about social issues, and cultural trends. Most important, the learning must create opportunities to "raise all voices" – to involve the greatest number of people possible in the conversation that ultimately will lead to a deeper sense of connection and belonging.

3. Connect

Understanding Israel as a resource for Jewish life establishes a foundation for mutuality and Peoplehood among world Jewry. Israel is a physical and spiritual space through which individuals connect to other Jews. Traditionally this has occurred through ceremony and ritual, whether through prayer, celebration of Israeli national holidays, or outpouring of support in times of war and turmoil and so on. The mutuality and meaning paradigm assumes the importance of these "mythological dimensions," but adds an additional building block.

A successful Israel education requires individuals to create a personally meaningful connection to Israel. Let your key stakeholders voice guide the content and direction of your educational work. If the educational program does not enable them to connect – to get excited, aggravated, passionate, motivated and interested, it cannot succeed.

✓ Key strategies for this purpose include:

- People-to-People programs in which Diaspora and Israeli Jews connect directly to one another, and in so doing make the relationship between Israel and the Diaspora, present at the personal level in an individual's life.

- Programs that connect locally, classrooms to classrooms, institutions to other institutions, one discipline to another.

- Connect to existing social networks in which rich and meaningful conversations about Israel and Jewish life among friends and colleagues are already commenting. If you can't find one, there are organizations with an interest to help you jump-start a network.

✓ These connecting strategies must bring intellectual and/or material benefit to the participants <u>and</u> your organization, otherwise don't get involved.

The vignettes and educator notes in this book provide many examples of the checked items listed above. We have tried to provide documentation of positive models for change in Israel education that can lead to a stronger sense of connection to Israel and deeper, more nuanced engagement with the multiple layers of the Land, People, and State. But, we also acknowledge that changing an educational paradigm is no easy task. The field and our state of knowledge is in a nascent stage. There are many obstacles and challenges that may impede implementation of the new paradigm, even when the will to do so is great.

We close with a brief description of a musical project that in many ways embodies all we have been striving to convey in this book. In 2010, the Israeli artist Kobi Oz released a CD entitled "*Mizmorei Nevuchim*" (Psalms for the Perplexed). The title reveals a lot about this endeavor. Oz comes from a Tunisian background and was raised in Sderot. Earlier in his musical career, he founded a band whose musical message was one of social commentary and critique. The band was called *Tipex*, whose name in Hebrew means "whiteout," in and of itself a critique against the European hegemony in Israeli culture and society, certainly a complicated topic worthy of exploration in and of itself. This more recent initiative reflects his journey to recover both his North African and his Jewish roots.

Oz's project is reflective of a trend among mainstream secular musicians in Israel that attempts to integrate Judaism into what it means to be Israeli. He seems to be trying to create a "usable present" by placing the old in conversation with the new, rather than just recasting of sacred music in a contemporary mode. In a couple of songs, he blends cuts from old cassette tapes of his grandfather singing *piyyut* (sacred poetry) with his modern musings on the meaning of secular prayer.[28] In another song called "Longing for Longings" he explores the Jewish condition of never quite being settled in any one place. The music is sometimes playful, sometimes poignant, and always pushing at questions of the relationship between being Israeli and being a Jew.

Oz appears to be trying to connect to the past in order to build a new Jewish future, even if it's a perplexing one as the CD title says. In his song, "*Elohai*" (my God), Oz seems to be expressing his Zionist dream when he writes:

But despite everything, tolerance is bubbling beneath the surface. Look how people are bit by bit leaving behind the tension. And in the end they just want to be united in this great synagogue called Eretz Yisrael.

Ultimately, that is our goal as well – to connect to the rich, complicated, often troublesome, always vibrant project of the Land, State, and People of Israel, through a sense of mutuality and meaning.

Amen, *sela* – may it be so in our day.

---

28 Elohai, with English sub-titles on
http://www.youtube.com/watch?v=ZUFWuEcykSg

REFERENCES

Ackerman, Walter. (1996). Israel in American Jewish Education. In Allon Gal (Ed.), *Envisioning Israel: The Changing Ideals and Images of North American Jews (pp. 173-190)*. Jerusalem and Detroit: The Magnes Press and Wayne State University Press.

Ament, Jonathon. (2005). *Israel Connections and American Jews, Report Series on the National Jewish Population Survey 2000-01*. New York: United Jewish Communities.

American Jewish Committee. (2003). *Annual survey of American Jewish opinion*. New York: American Jewish Committee.

Anderson, Benedict. (1991). *Imagined Communities: Reflections on the Origin and Spread of Nationalism*. New York: Verso.

Arbel, Andrea, S. (2010). *Partnership with a Purpose*. Jerusalem: The Jewish Agency for Israel.

Aron, Isa. (2000). *Becoming a Congregation of Learners: Learning as a Key to Revitalizing Congregations*. Vermont: Jewish Lights Press.

Aron, Isa, Cohen, Steven M., Hoffman, Steven M. & Kelman, Ari Y. (2010). *Sacred Strategies: Transforming Congregations from Functional to Visionary*. Washington, DC: Alban Publications.

Aviv, Caryn & Schneer, David. (2005). *New Jews: The End of the Jewish Diaspora*. New York: NYU Press.

Bar-On, Dan & Adwan, Sami (2006). The Prime Shared History Project. In Yaacov Iram, Hillel Wahrman & Zehavit Gross (Eds.), *Educating Toward a Culture of Peace* (pp.309-323). Information Age Publishing.

Bar-Shalom, Yehuda. (1998). *Encounters With the Other: An Ethnographic Study of the Mifgashim Programs for Jewish Youth, Summer 1997*. Jerusalem: The Charles R. Bronfman Centre for the Israel Experience.

Bar-Shalom, Yehuda. (2003). *Research Evaluation - Project Gvanim, The Development of Educational Centers on the Topic of Jewish Peoplehood in Teacher Training Colleges (Hebrew)*. Jerusalem: Research and Development Unit, Department of Jewish Zionist Education, The Jewish Agency for Israel.

Beinart, Peter. (2010). The Failure of the American Jewish Establishment. *New York Review of Books, June 10.* http://www.nybooks.com/articles/archives/2010/jun/10/failur e-american-jewish-establishment

Bekerman, Zvi & Kopelowitz, Ezra. (2007). The Unintended Consequence of Liberal Jewish Schooling: A Comparative Study of the Teaching of Jewish Texts for the Purpose of Cultural Sustainability. In Zvi Bekerman & Ezra Kopelowitz (Eds.), *Cultural Education-Cultural Sustainability - Minority, Diaspora, Indigenous and Ethno-Religious Groups in Multicultural Societies* (pp. 323-341) New York: Lawrence Erlbaum Publishers.

Bellah, Robert N., Madsen, Richard, Sullivan, William M., Swidler, Ann, Tipton, Steven M. (1985). *Habits of the Heart: Individualism and Commitment in American Life*. Berkeley: University of California Press.

Bialik, Haim. Nachman. (1922). Jewish Dualism. In: *Revealment and Concealment (pp. 22-24): Five Essays*. Jerusalem: Ibis (1st Editions), 2000.

Bram, Chen, & Neria, Eran. (2003a.) *Israeli Shlichim in American Jewish Summer Camps: The Meeting with a Different Religious World [Hebrew]*. Jerusalem: Research and Development Unit, Department of Jewish Zionist Education, The Jewish Agency for Israel.

Bram, Chen, & Neria, Eran (2003b). *Veni, Vedi, Ii: Israeli "Shlichim" Identity Encounters in U.S Jewish Summer camps [Hebrew]*. Jerusalem: Research and Development Unit, Department of Jewish Zionist Education, The Jewish Agency for Israel.

Brennan, Anne. (1980). Myth in Personal Spirituality. *Religious Education*, 75 (4), 441-451.

Brochstein, Laura Shulman & Bell Kligler, Roberta. (2008). *Best Practices Handbook: Boston-Haifa School to School Connections*. Boston: Combined Jewish Philanthropies.

Charmé, Stuart & Zelcowitz, Tali H. (2011). Educating for Jewish Identities: *Multiple Moving Targets. In Miller, Grant, & Pomson (Eds)*, *The International Handbook of Jewish Education* (163-181. Dordrecht: Springer.

Chazan, Barry. (1979). Israel in American Jewish schools revisited. *Jewish Education*, 42(2), 7-17.

Chazan, Barry. (1994). *The Israel Trip: A New Form of Jewish Education. Youth Trips to Israel: Rationale and Realization*. New York: CRB Foundation and The Mandell L. Berman Jewish Heritage Center at JESNA.

Chazan, Barry. (2002b). "The Philosophy of Informal Jewish Education," Paper commissioned by the Department of Jewish Zionist Education, The Jewish Agency for Israel.

Chazan, Barry. (2005). Schechter's lament: Israel and Jewish Education Once Again, *Agenda: Jewish Education*, 18.

Chertok, Fern, Sasson, Theodore & Saxe, Leonard. (2009). *Tourists, Travelers, and Citizens: Jewish Engagement of Young Adults in Four Centers of North American Jewish Life*. Boston: Cohen Center for Modern Jewish Studies, Brandeis University.

Cohen, E.H. (2008). *Youth Tourism to Israel: Educational Experiences of the Diaspora*. Channel View Publications.

Cohen, Steven M. (1998). *Religious stability and ethnic decline: Emerging patterns of Jewish identity in the United States*. New York: The Florence G. Heller – Jewish Community Centers Association Research Center.

Cohen, Steven M. & Eisen, Arnold M. (2000). *The Jew Within: Self, Family, and Community in America.* Bloomington, Indiana: Indiana University Press.

Cohen, Steven, M. & Kelman, Ari Y. (2006). *Beyond Distancing: Young Adults Jews and Their Relationship to Israel.* Report prepared for The Jewish Identity Project of Reboot, Andrea and Charles Bronfman Philanthropies.

Cohen, Steven M. & Kelman, Ari Y. (2007). *The continuity of discontinuity: How young American Jews are connecting, creating and organizing their own Jewish lives.* Andrea and Charles Bronfman Philanthropies.

Cohen, Steven M. & Kelman, Ari Y. (2010). Thinking About Distancing from Israel. *Contemporary Jewry*, 30 (2-3), 287-296.

Cohen, Steven M. & Kopelowitz, Ezra . (2010). *Journeys to Israel: The impact of longer-term programs upon Jewish Engagement & Israel Attachment.* Jerusalem: The Jewish Agency for Israel.

Cohen, Steven M., Kopelowitz, Ezra, Ukeles, Jack & Wolf, Minna. (2010). Assessing the Impact of Senior Jewish Educators and Campus Entrepreneurs Initiative Interns on the Jewish Engagement of College Students: Two year summary (2008-2010). *Hillel the Foundation for Jewish Campus Life and the Jim Joseph Foundation.*

Cohen, Steven M. & Melchior, Eitan. (2011). *The Jewish Learning Presence in JCC Day Camps: The Current Reality & Realizing the Potential.* New York: Florence G. Heller-JCCA Research Center.

Cohen, Steven. M. & Wall, Susan. (1994). *Excellence in Youth Trips to Israel. Youth Trips to Israel: Rationale and Realization.* New York: CRB Foundation and The Mandell L. Berman Jewish Heritage Center at JESNA.

DellaPergola, Sergio. (2010). Distancing, Yet One. *Contemporary Jewry*, 30 (2-3),183-190.

Dewey, John. (1992). My Pedagogic Creed. In K. Ryan and J. Cooper (Eds.), *Kaleidoscope: Readings in education* (pp. 363-369). Boston: Houghton Mifflin. (Originally published in 1897).

Diner, Hasia, Shandler, Jeffrey & Wenger, Beth S. (Eds). (2000). *Remembering the Lower East Side: American Jewish reflections.* Bloomington: Indiana University Press.

Ezrachi, Elan. (1994). *Encounters Between American Jews and Israelis: Israelis in American Summer Camps (Doctoral disseration).* The Graduate School of the Jewish Theological Seminary of America, New York.

Feldman, Jackie, & Katz, Neta. (2002). *The Place of the Jewish Agency in Mifgashim Between Israeli and Diaspora Youth: Cultural Differences, Administrative Practices and Hidden Ideological Positions.* Jerusalem: Department of Education, The Jewish Agency for Israel [Hebrew].

Gans, Herbert J. (1994). Symbolic ethnicity and symbolic religiosity: Towards a comparison of ethnic and religious acculturation. *Ethnic and Racial Studies*, 17(4), pp. 577-592.

Geffen, Peter. (2008). Israel Education: An Ironic Failure. *Sh'ma, A Journal of Social Responsibility*, 4-5.

Gordis, Daniel. (2009). *Saving Israel.* Hoboken, NJ: John Wiley & Sons.

Grant, Lisa D. (2001). The Role of Mentoring in Enhancing Experience of a Congregational Israel Trip. *Journal of Jewish Education*, 67 (1/2), 46-60.

Grant, Lisa D. (2006). *Yachdav/School-to-School Israel-Diaspora Virtual Mifgash Preliminary Program Evaluation.* Lokey International Academy of Jewish Studies at the Leo Baeck Education Center, Haifa, Israel.

Grant, Lisa D. (2007). Israel Education in Reform Congregational Schools. *CCAR Journal* LIV/III, 3-24.

Grant, Lisa D. (2008). Sacred Vision, Complex Reality: Navigating Tensions in Israel Education. *Jewish Educational Leadership*, 7(1), 22-2.

Grant, Lisa D. & Ezra Kopelowitz. (2009). *Strengthening the Connection of American Jews to Israel: A case study of one attempt to transform the place of Israel in four St. Louis congregations.* Paper presented at the Melton Centre for Jewish Education Israel Education Conference, December 2009.

Grant, Lisa D. (2011). Pluralistic Approaches to Israel Education, *Journal of Jewish Education*, 77:1, 4-21.

Grant, Lisa D. & Shlomi Ravid. (2011). Creating a Sustainable Sense of Peoplehood – Towards a Pedagogy of Commitment. *Jewish Educational Leadership*, 9 (2), 4-7.

Gringras, Robbie. (2008). An Ancient Dream & Modern Reality. *Sh'ma, A Journal of Social Responsibility, 19.*

Grishaver, Joel & Barkin, Josh. (2008). *Arzeinu: An Israel Encounter.* Los Angeles: Torah Aura Productions.

Horenczyk, Gabriel & Zvi Bekerman. (1997). The Effects of Intercultural Acquaintance and Structured Intergroup Interaction on Ingroup, Outgroup, and Reflected Ingroup Stereotypes. *International Journal of Intercultural Relationships*, 21, 71-83.

Horowitz, Bethamie. (2000). *Connections and Journeys: Assessing Critical Opportunities for Enhancing Jewish identity.* New York: UJA-Federation.

Hyman, Tali. (2008). *The Liberal Jewish Day School as Laboratory for Dissonance in American-Jewish Identity Formation.* Ph.D. Dissertation, New York: Steinhardt School of Culture, Education, and Human Development. New York.

Isaacs, Alick. (2011). The Purposes and Practices of Israel Education. In H. Miller, L. Grant, and A. Pomson, (Eds). *The*

International Handbook of Jewish Education (pp. 479-496). Dordrecht: Springer.

iCenter. (2012). *Mapping the Landscape of Israel Education.* Chicago: iCenter.

Israel, Steve. (2008). Teaching Israel, Teaching Truth: A Personal View from the Front. *Jewish Educational Leadership, 7*(1), 32-36.

Kaufman, David. (1999). *Shul with a Pool: The "Synagogue-Center" in American Jewish History.* Boston: Brandeis University Press.

Kelner, Shaul. (2002). *Almost Pilgrims: Authenticity, Identity and the Extra-Ordinary on a Jewish Tour of Israel (Doctoral disseration).* City University of New York, New York.

Kelner, Shaul. (2010). *Tours that Bind: Diaspora, Pilgrimage, and Israeli Birthright Tourism.* New York: NYU Press.

Kopelowitz, Ezra. (2003). *Between Mifgash and Shlichut: Paradigms in Contemporary Zionist Education and the Question of the Ideological Relationship between Israel and the Diaspora.* Jerusalem: Department of Jewish Zionist Education, The Jewish Agency.

Kopelowitz, Ezra. (2005). *Towards What Ideal Do We Strive? A Portrait of Social and Symbolic Israel Engagement in Community Day Schools.* Research report for the RAVSAK: The Jewish Community Day School Network and The Jewish Agency for Israel.

Kopelowitz, Ezra. (2007). *A Framework for Strategic Thinking about Jewish Peoplehood.* Tel Aviv: Nadav Foundation.

Kopelowitz, Ezra. (2010b). *The Tri-Center Project--Two Years Later.* World Confederation of Jewish Community Centers. Jerusalem, Israel.

Kopelowitz, Ezra & Ravid, Shlomi. (2010). Best Practices of Organizations that build Jewish Peoplehood: A Policy-Oriented

Analysis of a Field in Formation. Jerusalem: Nadav Foundation and the Jewish Peoplehood HUB.

Kopelowitz, Ezra, Wolf, Minna & Markowitz, Stephen. (2009). *High School Israel Experience Programs: A Policy-Oriented Analysis of the Field.* Jerusalem: The Jewish Agency for Israel.

Kujawski, Nina. (2000). *Building Interpersonal Relations through Mifgashim (*Unpublished Final Project). Senior Educators Program, Melton Centre for Jewish Education, The Hebrew University of Jerusalem, Jerusalem.

Lehmann, Daniel. (2008). Calling Integration into Question: A Discourse Analysis of English and Humash Classes at a Modern Orthodox Yeshiva High School. *Journal of Jewish Education,* 74(3), 295-316.

Liebman, Charles & Cohen, Steven M. (1990). *Two Worlds of Judaism: The Israeli and American Experiences.* New Haven: Yale University Press.

Levisohn, Jon. (2008). From Integration of Curricula to the Pedagogy of Integrity. *Journal of Jewish Education,* 74(3), 264-294.

Lukinsky, Joseph. (1978). Integrating Jewish and General Studies in the Day School. In M. Nadel (Ed.), *Integrative learning: The Search for Unity in Jewish Day School Programs.* New York: American Association for Jewish Education.

Malkus, Mitch. (2001). *Portraits of curriculum integration in Jewish day schools (* Unpublished Doctoral dissertation). Jewish Theological Seminary, New York.

Malkus, Mitch (2011). Curriculum Integration. In H. Miller, L. D. Grant, and A. Pomson (Eds.), *The International Handbook of Jewish Education* (pp. 83-97). Dordrecht: Springer

Margolis, Daniel (2008). Towards a Vision of Educational Re-Engagement with Israel in Day Schools. *Jewish Educational Leadership,* 7 (1),17-21.

Marmur, Michael. (2007). Happiness inside the State: Towards a Liberal Theology of Israel. *CCAR Journal*, LIV:II, 24-30.

Mittelberg, David. (2011). Jewish Peoplehood Education. In H. Miller, L. Grant, L. and A. Pomson (Eds). *The International Handbook of Jewish Education* (pp. 515-539). Dordrecht: Springer.

Meyer, Michael. (2003). Reflections on the Educated Jew from the Perspective of Reform Judaism. In Fox, Scheffler & Marom (Eds), *Visions of Jewish Education* (pp. 122-177). Cambridge: Cambridge University Press

Neria, Eran. (2003). *Interviews with Adi and Amir: Israeli Counselors in American Jewish Summer Camps [Hebrew]*. Jerusalem: Research and Development Unit, Department of Jewish Zionist Education, The Jewish Agency.

Nisan, Mordecai. (2009). *Emotion and Cognition in the Development of Jewish Identity in the Individual: A Psychological Inquiry*. Jerusalem: Mandel Foundation.

Nussbaum, Martha C. (1997). *Cultivating humanity: A classical defense of reform in liberal education*. Cambridge, MA: Harvard University Press.

Oz, Amos. (1981). *To Love the Land with Humility* (Hebrew). Speech delivered to the Society for the Protection of Nature in Israel.

Perlman, Lee. (2008). Commitment and Critique: A Paradigm Shift. *Sh'ma, A Journal of Social Responsibility*, February/March, 16-17.

Peters, Richard S. (1970). *Ethics and education*. London, UK: Allen and Unwin.

Pomson, Alex. (2001). "Knowledge that doesn't just sit there: Considering a reconceptualization of the curriculum integration of Jewish and general studies." *Religious Education*, 96(4), 528-545.

Pomson, Alex & Deitcher, Howard. (2010). Day School Education in the Age of Birthright. *Journal of Jewish Education*. 76 (1), 52-73.

Pomson, Alex, Deitcher, Howard, & Muszkat-Barkan, Michal. (2009). *Israel education in North American Day Schools: A systems analysis and some strategies for change*. Report submitted to the Avi Chai Foundation.

Pomson, Alex & Grant, Lisa D. (2004). Getting Personal with Professional Development: The Case of Short-term Trips to Israel for Diaspora Teachers. In Joseph Bashi, Miriam Ben Peretz & Ami Bouganim (Eds.), *Education and Professional Training*. Jerusalem: The Jewish Agency for Israel.

Portes, Alejaro & Robert D. Manning. (2012). The Immigrant Enclave: Theory and Empirical Examples. In Jan Lin & Christopher Mele (Eds.), (pp. 152-163) *The Urban Sociology Reader*, New York: Routledge.

Putnam, Robert. (2001). *Bowling Alone: The Collapse and Revival of American Community*. New York: Simon & Schuster.

Reimer, Joseph. (1997). *Succeeding at Jewish Education*. Philadelphia: Jewish Publication Society of America.

Reinharz, Jehuda. (2003). *Israel in the eyes of Americans: A call for action*. Waltham, MA: Cohen Center for Modern Jewish Studies, Brandeis University.

Roof, Wade Clark. (2001). *Spiritual Marketplace: Baby Boomers and the Remaking of American Religion*. Princeton: Princeton University Press.

Sales, Amy L., Nicole Samuel & Matthew Boxer. (2011). *Limud by the Lake Revisited: Growth and Change at Jewish Summer Camp*. Boston: Maurice & Marilyn Cohen Center for Modern Jewish Studies (CMJS).

Sarna, Jonathan. (1996). A Projection of America as it Ought to be: Zion in the Mind's Eye of American Jews. In Allon Gal (Ed.), *Envisioning Israel: The Changing Ideals and Images of North American Jews (pp. 41-69)*. Detroit: Wayne State University Press.

Sasson, Theodore. (2010). The Mass Mobilization to Direct Engagement. *Israel Studies*, 15 (1), pp. 173-195.

Sasson, Theodore, Kadushin, Charles, & Saxe, Leonard. (2008). *American Jewish Attachment to Israel: An Assessment of the 'Distancing' Hypothesis, Steinhardt Social Research Institute, at the Maurice and Marilyn Cohen Center for Modern Jewish Studies*. Boston: Brandeis University.

Sasson, Theodore, Mittelberg, David, Hecht, Shahar & Saxe, Leonard. (2008). *Encountering the Other, Finding Oneself: The Taglit-Birthright Israel Mifgash*. Maurice and Marilyn Cohen Center for Modern Jewish Studies, Brandeis University.

Sasson, Theodore, Phillips, Benjamin, Wright, Graham, Kadushin, Charles & Saxe, Leonard. (2010). *Birth Cohort Differences in Israel Attachment: Generational Versus Lifecycle Effects*. Cohen Center for Modern Jewish Studies, Brandeis University.

Sasson, Theodore, Phillips, Benjamin, Wright, Graham, Kadushin, Charles & Saxe, Leonard. (2012). Understanding Young Adult Attachment to Israel: Period, Lifecycle and Generational Dynamics. *Contemporary Jewry*, 32 (1), 67-84.

Saxe, Leonard & Chazan, Barry. (2008). *Ten Days of Birthright Israel: A Journey in Young Adult Identity*. Boston: Brandeis University Press.

Schön, Donald. (1995). *The Reflective Practitioner: How Professionals Think in Action*. Ashgate Publishing.

Shulman, Lee S. (1987). Knowledge and Teaching: Foundations of the New Reform. *Harvard Educational Review*, 57 (1), 1-22.

Sinclair, Alex. (2011). Practitioner Enquiry and its Role in Jewish Education. In H. Miller, L. Grant, and A. Pomson (Eds.), *The International Handbook of Jewish Education (pp. 917-936)*. Dordrecht: Springer.

Solomon, Bennet. (1978). A Critical Review of the Term Integration in the Literature of the Jewish Day School in America. *Jewish Education* 46 (4), 24-48.

Stein, Kenneth. (2009). What Works in Israel education. Hayidion. RAVSAK: The Jewish Community Day School Network, Spring.

Tanchel, Susan. (2006). *Honoring Voices: Listening to the Texts and the Teacher, the Scholars and the Students : A Study in the Uses of Subject Matter Knowledge of Tanakh in the Contexts of Research and Teaching* (Unpublished Doctoral dissertation). Brandeis University, Waltham, MA.

Ukeles, Jacob, Miller, Ron & Beck, Pearl. (2006). *Young Jewish Adults in the United States Today: Harbingers of the American Jewish Community of Tomorrow?* Report prepared for the American Jewish Committee (AJC).

Wertheimer, Jack (Editor). (2009). *Learning and Community: Jewish Supplementary Schools in the Twenty-First Century*. Boston: Brandeis University Press.

Wiener, Julie. (2010). "New Consensus Seen Emerging on Israel Education." *The Jewish Week*, December 7. http://www.thejewishweek.com/news/new_york/new_consens us_seen_emerging_israel_education.

Wolf, Minna F. (2007). *Adjusting the Boundary: Exploring Identities during Israel Experience Mifgashim* (Unpublished Doctoral dissertation). Melton Centre for Jewish Education, The Hebrew University of Jerusalem, Jerusalem.

Wolf, Minna F. & Kopelowitz, Ezra. (2003). *Israeli Staff in American Jewish Summer Camps- The View of the Camp Director.*

Jerusalem: Department of Jewish Zionist Education, The Jewish Agency for Israel.

Wuthnow, Robert. (2010). *After the Baby Boomers: How Twenty- and Thirty-Somethings Are Shaping the Future of American Religion.* Princeton: Princeton University Press.

Yachdav: School-to-School Israel-Diaspora Virtual Mifgash Program. Jerusalem: The Israel Movement for Progressive Judaism. RationalYachdav-1.pdf (On-line brochure).

Zakai, Sivan. (2011). "Values in Tension: Israel Education at a U.S. Jewish Day School," *Journal of Jewish Education*, 77:3, 239-265.

Zelda, (2004). *The Spectacular Difference: Selected Poems.* Marcia Falk, (trans.) Cincinnati: Hebrew Union College Press.

Zeldin, Michael. (1992). To See the World as Whole: The Promise of the Integrated Curriculum. *Jewish Education News*, 13 (3), 13.

INDEX

B

Birthright · 13, 42, 45, 46, 54, 63, 68, 69, 90, 97, 99, 151, 154, 155

C

Camp · 2, 3, 22, 50, 64, 101, 102, 103, 121, 123, 124, 125, 126, 127, 129, 130, 131, 132, 133, 135, 154
ceremony · 6, 17, 20, 21, 23, 24, 25, 26, 27, 56, 69, 104, 122, 143
Cohen · 12, 13, 14, 15, 20, 42, 43, 46, 63, 101, 146, 148, 149, 152, 154, 155
communities · 5, 10, 51, 60, 90, 94, 95, 96, 97, 98, 99, 100, 109, 113, 115, 120, 124
community · 8, 11, 12, 13, 14, 21, 22, 23, 25, 29, 31, 32, 33, 34, 35, 36, 37, 39, 40, 41, 42, 43, 45, 50, 51, 55, 58, 71, 76, 77, 79, 81, 82, 83, 85, 86, 88, 90, 93, 94, 95, 100, 103, 104, 107, 108, 111, 113, 116, 120, 127, 129
congregation · 14, 33, 34, 35, 36, 40, 41, 48, 51, 52

connections · 4, 18, 21, 35, 40, 41, 55, 66, 69, 72, 73, 85, 93, 94, 95, 96, 100, 101, 105, 107, 113, 114, 119, 126, 132, 133, 135, 137, 138
Conservative · 33, 35, 51, 64, 95, 102, 103, 117
culture · 16, 17, 20, 21, 24, 29, 30, 31, 32, 35, 48, 49, 50, 62, 67, 71, 76, 80, 83, 89, 98, 111, 114, 119, 122, 123, 124, 131, 132, 136, 138, 141, 144
curriculum · 13, 20, 25, 26, 29, 30, 48, 49, 51, 52, 66, 71, 74, 82, 86, 88, 91, 92, 95, 96, 107, 108, 110, 111, 112, 113, 114, 115, 116, 126, 127, 128, 131, 138, 152, 153, 156

D

Diaspora · 3, 5, 6, 7, 8, 9, 12, 13, 15, 16, 18, 42, 51, 55, 56, 59, 68, 69, 77, 91, 94, 96, 97, 98, 100, 101, 102, 105, 107, 108, 114, 115, 116, 117, 127, 140, 143, 146, 147, 148, 149, 150, 151, 154

E

educator · *18, 20, 34, 53, 55, 87, 91, 108, 128, 129, 135, 143*

engagement · *6, 10, 12, 13, 17, 18, 21, 31, 32, 33, 34, 36, 37, 39, 40, 41, 42, 44, 46, 49, 50, 52, 54, 56, 57, 58, 66, 67, 73, 74, 85, 89, 91, 95, 100, 107, 111, 112, 122, 125, 128, 139, 140, 141, 142, 144*

Eretz · *51, 59, 62, 67, 131, 137, 144*

F

Federation · *14, 33, 52, 95, 96, 119, 150, 151*

Focus Israel · *33*

G

Grant · *1, 9, 16, 20, 45, 46, 48, 50, 55, 60, 63, 88, 95, 107, 112, 124, 147, 150, 151, 152, 153, 154, 155*

H

Harlam · *3, 22, 50, 121, 124, 125, 126, 127, 128, 130, 131, 133, 136, 139*

Hatikvah · *24*

Hebrew · *2, 9, 21, 22, 25, 27, 29, 30, 31, 32, 49, 52, 57,* *58, 60, 63, 66, 83, 91, 92, 97, 101, 103, 104, 110, 122, 123, 124, 130, 131, 135, 144, 146, 147, 149, 152, 153, 156*

I

identity · *9, 12, 14, 15, 24, 32, 36, 43, 52, 53, 54, 55, 61, 62, 65, 68, 88, 90, 97, 100, 102, 105, 107, 109, 111, 122, 123, 124, 125, 127, 128, 130, 135, 140, 148, 150, 151*

integration · *27, 29, 32, 40, 48, 49, 50, 52, 86, 99, 103, 104, 105, 110, 117, 121, 125, 127, 130, 135, 137, 138, 141, 152, 153, 155*

Israel advocacy · *6, 7, 15, 20, 77, 88, 89*

Israel education · *4, 5, 6, 7, 8, 9, 10, 12, 13, 14, 15, 16, 17, 19, 20, 21, 22, 26, 27, 40, 42, 48, 50, 54, 56, 71, 74, 76, 77, 79, 82, 83, 85, 86, 87, 88, 89, 90, 93, 94, 96, 97, 100, 101, 114, 115, 116, 121, 122, 123, 124, 125, 126, 127, 128, 129, 130, 132, 133, 136, 138, 139, 140, 141, 143, 153, 155*

Israel Experience · *42, 43, 146, 147, 149, 152, 156*

Israeli flag · *20, 23, 111*

J

Jewish Agency · *15, 33, 51, 59, 89, 94, 95, 101, 102, 121, 146, 147, 148, 149, 151, 152, 153, 154, 156*
Judaism · *4, 8, 12, 16, 17, 21, 43, 52, 55, 57, 60, 61, 62, 80, 92, 107, 108, 121, 123, 125, 128, 134, 137, 138, 140, 144, 152, 153*

K

Knesset Israel · 33, 36, 41
Kopelowitz · *1, 12, 14, 16, 20, 22, 24, 42, 45, 46, 49, 95, 98, 99, 101, 102, 103, 104, 147, 148, 149, 150, 151, 152, 156*

L

L'om · *59, 60*
Leadership · *2, 9, 33, 52, 100, 141, 150, 151, 153*

M

MAKOM · *33, 51, 52*
Medinah · *51, 67*
Mifgash
   mifgashim · *2, 3, 97, 98, 107, 150, 151, 155*
mutuality · *4, 6, 15, 18, 53, 74, 140, 143, 145*

P

People · *2, 7, 8, 12, 14, 35, 43, 45, 56, 57, 59, 85, 90, 93, 94, 95, 127, 138, 141, 142, 143, 144*
Peoplehood · *5, 19, 45, 50, 60, 98, 99, 100, 115, 124, 126, 136, 143, 146, 150, 151, 152, 153*
Pesach · *113*

R

RAVSAK · *22, 23, 24, 25, 151, 155*
Reform · *33, 50, 51, 57, 58, 61, 66, 67, 68, 69, 70, 88, 95, 102, 103, 121, 123, 124, 128, 134, 136, 137, 150, 153, 155*
religious · *4, 7, 11, 12, 14, 16, 17, 21, 24, 26, 29, 39, 51, 57, 58, 61, 66, 70, 72, 73, 79, 80, 87, 88, 89, 92, 102, 111, 130, 136, 138, 149*
research · *5*
ruach · 127, 128

S

Shabbat · *4, 61, 123*

T

teaching · *9, 10, 16, 18, 25, 45, 53, 55, 69, 71, 81, 85, 87, 88, 89, 91, 114, 127, 133, 136, 138, 155*
Tefila · *123*
tikkun middot · *129*
tikkun olam · *129*
Torah · *4, 8, 49, 51, 67, 128, 134, 150*
Tu B'Shvat · *111*

V

Vignette · *2, 3, 22, 29, 33, 42, 48, 49, 50, 59, 63, 71,* *76, 85, 86, 95, 97, 101, 107, 114, 121, 128*

Y

Yachdav · *3, 107, 108, 110, 111, 112, 113, 115, 150*
Yom Ha'atzmaut · *111*

Z

Zionism · *5, 10, 43, 63, 64, 65, 67, 68, 70, 80, 137, 138*

Made in the USA
Lexington, KY
15 April 2015